FORGETTING

Gabriel Josipovici was born in Nice in 1940 of Russo-Italian, Romano-Levantine parents. He lived in Egypt from 1945 to 1956, when he came to Britain. He is the author of eighteen novels, three volumes of short stories, nine critical works, and numerous stage and radio plays, and is a regular contributor to the *Times Literary Supplement*. His plays have been performed throughout Britain and on radio in Britain, France and Germany, and his work has been translated into the major European languages and Arabic. In 2016, Carcanet published *The Teller and the Tale: Essays on Literature and Culture, 1990–2015*.

FORGETTING

GABRIEL JOSIPOVICI

LITTLE ISLAND PRESS

in collaboration with Carcanet

First published in Great Britain in 2020 by
Little Island Press / Carcanet
Alliance House, 30 Cross Street
Manchester M2 7AQ
www.carcanet.co.uk

A CIP catalogue record for this book is
available from the British Library.
ISBN 978 1 78410 890 8

Book design by Andrew Latimer
Printed in Great Britain by SRP Ltd, Exeter, Devon

MIX
Paper from
responsible sources
FSC
www.fsc.org   FSC® C014540

Supported using public funding by the National Lottery
through Arts Council England.

Supported using public funding by
ARTS COUNCIL
ENGLAND

CONTENTS

In Memory of George Craig

*In her dream Mrs Devonshire saw two men approach.
As they drew near one of them leant towards her
and said in a low voice: 'You think we haven't
forgotten you, but we have.' Then she woke up.*

It wasn't till I started writing this preface that I realised how much my thoughts had turned to questions of memory and its secret sharer, forgetting, in the past twenty-five years. In 1993 I wrote a play for radio called *The Museum of Forgetfulness*. It was when museums were springing up everywhere on the South Bank, and I was intrigued by the paradox of a museum, a building dedicated to storing a nation's treasures so that they can be looked at by all and so kept in the national memory, being devoted to the opposite, forgetting; and by the problem of how to represent forgetting, since by representing it one denies it. Then in 1998 I was invited to give a talk at a conference on the Holocaust and Memory, organised by the German-Jewish Centre at the University of Sussex. The result was a piece which I entitled 'Memory: Too Little/Too Much' and where I explored the notion that the slogan 'We must never forget!' is as dangerous as it is vital – vital because the terrible things that happened to Europe in the years 1933–45 must indeed not be allowed to disappear from memory – but dangerous because that phrase can so easily be used by demagogues to stir up hatred. For as Tom Sharpe puts it in one of his South African novels, 'Heroes Day provided everyone with an opportunity to forget the present and revive old hatreds.' The problem of forgetting is more than a conceptual paradox.

Over the next two decades, like so many of my generation, I found myself comforting friends whose spouses or parents had succumbed to Alzheimer's or dementia, and watching the effects of this disease on families and individuals. Then, in 2015, as I was finishing a book on *Hamlet*, I realised to my astonishment that it touched on many of the issues I had been turning over in my mind in connection with both the public and the private aspects of memory and forgetting: how to lay the past to rest; what constitutes a person; whether it's possible to know what one feels, and so on. And it seemed to be no accident that *Hamlet* was written and performed around 1600, just when in Europe the transition from medieval to modern was accelerating. Any discussion of memory and forgetting, I sensed, should be, must be, conducted with an awareness of changing cultural landscapes.

At the same time, I felt very strongly that all attempts at a historical or cultural exploration of memory and forgetting had to acknowledge the fact that each person's mode of remembering and forgetting is subject to personal, generic, cultural and historical imperatives. Thus I decided to introduce interludes into the text at key junctures to jolt the reader into contemplating specific cases of the anguished interconnectedness of the need to forget and the fear of forgetting.

I would like to thank all those who have contributed to this book. First my mother for helping me to understand the importance of both remembering and forgetting in life, and for providing the anecdote I have used as epigraph and the one which opens section eight. Sadly, she did not live to read either the lecture on the Holocaust and memory or the *Hamlet* book, on both of which I would have welcomed her views. Rosalind Belben, Steve Mitchelmore, Giglia Sprigge, Bernard Sharratt and Tamar Miller all read drafts of the book and made detailed and perceptive comments on it, some of which saved me from error or made me think again about how best to put my argument and some of which I chose to ignore, perhaps to the detriment of the finished work. To all, and especially to Tamar, who has been a supportive presence for as long as the book has been in gestation, I am profoundly grateful.

Lewes
April 2019

I

THE FEAR OF FORGETTING

Today, we are terrified of forgetting.

Suddenly, it seems, Alzheimer's is all around us. Few of us do not have relatives or friends who have been struck down by the disease, living proof of its deadly power. And everyone over sixty finds him or herself constantly checking for evidence that it has not (yet) got hold of him or her.

The disease was only recognised in the early years of the last century, barely a hundred years ago. Previously it had been elided with senility: when you got old you lost, among other things, your memory, and in some cases this was more pronounced than in others. Then in 1901 Dr Alois Alzheimer, a senior physician at the Frankfurt Hospital for the Epileptic and the Mentally Ill, was alerted to the case of a fifty-one-year-old woman, Auguste B., who had been admitted to the hospital by her husband, who had found himself unable to cope any longer with her inexplicable outbursts of rage and increasingly alarming memory lapses. By 1904, three years after her admission to the hospital, Frau Auguste was bedridden, permanently curled up in a foetal position, her knees drawn up to her chest, muttering, unable to speak, and needing assistance to eat. She died in April 1906.

Though he had by then moved to Munich to work with the renowned psychiatrist, Emil Kraepelin, as soon as Dr Alzheimer learned of Frau Auguste's death he put in a request to be allowed to examine her corpse. Because of recent advances in medical technology he was able to do what had not been possible before, to examine the brain of the victim of a terrible and mysterious illness. What he and his assistants found in the cerebral cortex was what a recent writer on the subject has described thus:

> The cortex was speckled with crusty brown clumps – plaques – too many to count. They varied in size, shape and texture, and seemed to be a hodge-podge of granules and short, crooked threads, as if they were sticky magnets for microscopic trash.[1]

At the same time, in the second and third layers of the cortex nearly a third of the neurons had been obliterated, overrun with what Alzheimer called 'a tangled bundle of fibrils'. These are the ordinary components of every neuron, but in Frau Auguste's brain they had grown out of all proportion, destroying everything within their reach.

That was in 1906. A century later and despite huge advances in medicine and neuro-science we still know far too little about the disease, even though it now seems to be all around us.[2] Yet it was only in the 1970s that countries in the West began to realise that unless some sort of cure was found the strain on medical and social resources would become almost impossible for society to bear. This is because, though Alzheimer's is now understood as qualitatively different from the forgetfulness

---

1   David Schenk, *The Forgetting* (London; 2001), p.24.

2   Though both plaques and tangles are usually to be found in the brains of patients with Alzheimer's, it's now clear that this is not always the case and there are also examples of people who do not suffer from the disease who have them. In recent years too the glass plates Alzheimer and his team produced of Frau Auguste's brain have been found, so that scientists and scholars can now see what he saw and do not have to rely simply on his reports. From this new evidence it appears that hers was a rather rare form of the disease. None of this, though, has changed the general picture.

and absent-mindedness that naturally overtakes the elderly, it is nevertheless a disease whose likelihood increases with age, and, as advances in medicine since the war have led to a population that lives ever longer, the incidence of Alzheimer's has increased dramatically. Unfortunately, though hardly a month goes by without a newspaper headline proclaiming that a cure has been found, there is no sign yet of any solution to the problem of how to stop or reverse it.

Scientific description of the condition tells us nothing of what it feels like to inhabit it. And it is obvious that if you suffer from it you are unlikely to be able to describe it. Writers over the past half century have tried to imagine it, with more or less plausibility. One of the finest such attempts, to my mind, is by the French writer Jean Echenoz in his extraordinary little novel, *Ravel*. The musician probably suffered from the condition towards the end of his life (it has even been suggested that the compulsive repetitive nature of *Bolero* is proof of this), and Echenoz brings home to the reader how part of the horror, for him, was his awareness of what was happening:

If he no longer recognises most people, he is aware of everything. He sees clearly that his movements no longer achieve their purpose, that he grabs a knife by its blade, that he brings to his lips the lighted end of his cigarette only to quickly correct himself – no, he murmurs to himself, not like that. He knows that one doesn't cut one's nails like this, that one doesn't put on one's glasses that way, and, if he nevertheless dons them to read *Le Populaire*, the muscles of his eyes no longer allow him to follow the lines. He sees all this clearly, the subject of his fall as well as its attentive spectator, buried alive in a body that no longer responds to his intellect, watching a stranger live within him.[3]

---

3   Jean Echenoz, *Ravel*, Paris, 2006, pp.116–7. My translation.

Emerson, the great nineteenth-century American essayist who also probably suffered from Alzheimer's in later life, summed up the common view of the role of memory in our lives in his essay on the subject. Without memory, he said, 'all life and thought were an unrelated succession. Memory holds together past and present... and gives continuity and dignity to human life. It holds us to our family, to our friends. Hereby a home is possible, hereby a new fact has value.' The peculiar horror for the family and friends of the victim of Alzheimer's stems from the fact that our loved ones are still there, looking as they have always looked, moving, for the most part, as they have always moved, occasionally even talking as they have always talked, But because they are starting to forget – forget what has just happened or been said to them, as well as large chunks of their past – we feel that they are only intermittently 'with' us. In many cases there are violent outbursts and even aggressive behaviour, as though the person has not just forgotten who they are but even what it means to be a human being. A line has been crossed and even the victim knows that it can never be crossed back again.

*

It was probably not the sudden increase in the observed cases of Alzheimer's in the seventies that first alerted the general public in Britain and America to the fact that we had in our midst men and women like ourselves in every way except that they had lost the ability to remember, but rather the publication of a book that was not about Alzheimer's disease at all. This was Oliver Sacks's *Awakenings*.

Sacks was a young British neurologist working in a New York hospital when the book came out in 1973. Its subject matter was extraordinary and it was written with a passion and a command of language unusual in a scientific book. Indeed, it was the literary rather than the medical establishment which first recognised its merits. It had been rather frostily received by the medical establishment on its first appearance, leading Sacks, in the second edition published by Penguin three years later, to develop, often in footnotes, where exactly he felt at odds with received medical wisdom. The copious quotations from writers in this edition, especially the two seventeenth-century writers, John Donne and Thomas Browne, who both wrote about illness, show him growing in confidence in the articulation of the larger picture. He argues that medicine, since the time of Donne and Browne, had made great strides by focussing on the body as a machine, but had in the process forgotten that the body is first and foremost an organism, a whole, and should be treated as such. Donne and Browne, religious men in a religious age, had a strong sense of the interconnection of the physical and the spiritual and thought it quite natural to invoke notions such as soul and repentance in connection with illness, and this struck Sacks as truer to his observations as a neurologist than the obsession of the medical profession only with observable phenomena. This obsession, he suggests, infects the very language with which we speak of disease and healing, thus subtly falsifying what we are attempting to understand. Seemingly neutral terms like 'silver bullets' and 'side-effects' suggest that something is central and something is peripheral, whereas the body is one and change, for better or worse, happens to the whole person.

So persuasive was Sacks's writing and so striking the subjects he was dealing with that in the intervening years, despite doubts being expressed over this or that detail of his method, those doctors who have been influenced by him and who have tried to carry on his work have become the mainstream of the profession. But back in the 60s Sacks was a young, unknown neurologist, working in Mount Carmel Hospital in the Bronx in New York, when he came across a group of patients the authorities had given up on. They were the victims of the great influenza epidemic (*encephalitis lethargica*) which had hit Europe and the United States in the years immediately after World War I and had left its victims (probably more numerous than the entirety of those who had died in the war) unable to cope with the demands of society. Many of them had ceased to be able to move or even speak. They haunted the homes of loving relatives who could afford to look after them and, for those with no such support or whose symptoms could not be coped with by their families, they haunted the hospitals and psychiatric institutions of the West. Sacks came across those who had ended up at Mount Carmel Hospital at exactly the same time as advances in medicine and technology made some sort of treatment conceivable. This was the development of the drug L-DOPA (L-3,4 – dihydroxyphenylalaline), described by him as 'a remarkable "awakening" drug'. He decided to administer it to his patients and see if he could bring these people, some of whom had been 'sleeping' for thirty years or more, back to life. His book describes what happened when he did so, first telling the story in general terms and then detailing the case histories of over a dozen patients.

Encephalitis lethargica is a form of Parkinson's disease. The patient appears to be locked into his or her body and movement ceases to be natural but becomes an ordeal, leading either to mad rushing or sudden stasis. As one patient tells him: 'I run out of space.'[4] This leads in time to a gradual withdrawal from the world and then a gradual forgetting of

---

4   One of Sacks's great gifts was his ability to listen to what the victims themselves were saying, and it was his good fortune and ours that the combination of extraordinary disease and new drug allowed the more imaginative and articulate of his patients to exist both inside and outside the condition at the same time and so be able to provide information 'from the other side'.

who or what one is. When Sacks first administered L-DOPA the effects were immediate and extraordinary. Euphoria, as the patients suddenly 'came alive', but also overexcitement and wildly unrealistic expectations. In every case the initial dosage had to be altered, depending on each patient's reaction, and then constantly monitored and adjusted until some sort of balance could be found between hyperactivity and relapse.

But this was not simply a case of physical adjustment. Far more important was the mental and emotional adjustments the patients were having to make to cope with this sudden brave new world. For one of the things they would have to confront was that they had in effect been asleep for, and therefore lost for ever, the greater part of their lives. The case studies describe how different patients deal with this – having a loving family taking an interest in them, for example, was a huge help, while being quite alone in the world made things that much harder.

Perhaps the most extreme case was that of Rose R., born in 1905 in New York City into a wealthy and talented family. High-spirited and fun-loving, she lived her youthful years in a social whirl, partying, flying aeroplanes (the new craze among the very rich), and developing her considerable gifts for drawing. Then, at the age of twenty-one, she was struck down by a violent form of *encephalitis lethargica*, one of its last victims before the epidemic vanished in 1926 as mysteriously as it had arrived. She lost the ability to speak, had difficulty with balance and developed other signs of Parkinsonism. In 1935 her ageing parents reluctantly committed her to Mount Carmel Hospital. There her state hardly changed for thirty years, and when Sacks first saw her in 1966, he writes, 'my findings coincided with the original notes from her admission'. As a staff-nurse said to him: 'It's uncanny, that woman hasn't aged a day in the thirty years I've known her. The rest of us get older – but Rosie's the same.' At sixty-one she looked thirty, with raven-black hair and a completely unlined face: her illness had preserved her intact.

L-DOPA, which Sacks began to administer in the summer of 1969, had an almost immediate effect on her. She began to walk unaided, to take part in normal conversations and even to show signs of cheerfulness. Sacks increased the dose and she continued to improve: 'It's fabulous! It's gorgeous!' she would call out to him in the idiom of a long-gone epoch. But then suddenly she was down, and in the succeeding days her moods fluctuated wildly, one moment telling jokes and even singing 'songs of an astonishing lewdness', as Sacks noted, the next growing gloomy and suspicious. 'Something awful is coming,' she told Sacks in one of those moods, and come it did. Not much more than a month after starting the course of L-DOPA her physical condition began to deteriorate, 'ticcing, jammed and blocked' in Sacks's startling formulation. Her involuntary brushing of her face with her hand became a compulsive and violent action, causing abrasure of the skin and bleeding. Soon she could neither move nor speak, 'During the last days of August,' he writes, 'Miss R seemed to be totally blocked in all spheres of activity: everything about her showed an extremity of tension, which was entirely prevented from finding an outlet. Her face at this time was continual clenched in a horrified, tortured and anguished expression. Her prediction of a month earlier was completely fulfilled: something awful had come, and it was as bad as they come.'[5]

Sacks kept her under observation, noting how visits from her family would 're-awaken' her and lead to momentary vivacity, making one realise what an intelligent and charming person she had once been. She was even able to talk to Sacks about that summer of 1969 and the transformation the initial use of L-DOPA had wrought in her. She knew perfectly well it was

---

5   Oliver Sacks, *Awakenings* (London; 1976), pp.101–13.

1969, she said, and that she was sixty-eight, but she felt it was 1926 and she was twenty-five. As Sacks sums up her tragic case:

> It seems, in retrospect, as if the L-DOPA must have deblocked her for a short while and revealed to her a time-gap beyond comprehension or bearing, and that she has subsequently been forced to 'reblock' herself and the possibility of any similar reaction to L-DOPA ever happening again. She continues to look much younger than her years, indeed, in a fundamental sense, she is much younger than her age. But she is a Sleeping Beauty, whose 'awakening' was unbearable to her, and who will never be woken again. (114–5)[6]

The fear of forgetting, then, and the fear of remembering are two sides of the same coin. After a certain age all of us in the West are terrified of forgetting who we are, forgetting the past that has made us who we are. But Rosie R. could not bear to remember because most of her life would then be revealed to be a blank, and she preferred to revert to this blankness for the remainder of her life.

*

A brief look at one of the earliest narratives known to us, Homer's *Odyssey*, will help to round out the picture. When the *Odyssey* opens the first thing we are told after a brief overture is that all those warriors who fought at Troy and survived have returned home, all apart from Odysseus:

---

6   Harold Pinter was so moved by her case that he wrote a short play based on it, *A Kind of Alaska*, memorably performed by Judy Dench at the National Theatre in 1992. A film of *Awakenings*, starring Robin Williams, was released in 1991, further extending the book's reach.

Odysseus alone, filled with longing for his return and for his wife (*nostou kechrêmenon êde gunaikos*), did the queenly nymph Calypso, that bright goddess, keep back in her hollow caves, yearning that he should be her husband. (i.13–14)[7]

The immortal nymph Calypso, whose name suggests she is the one who covers or hides (we are familiar with its opposite, apocalypse, that which will be revealed), has hidden him away in her caves and despite his protestations, keeps him imprisoned on her island out of love for him. And when we first encounter him, five books later, it is in the classic posture of longing, 'sitting on the shore, and his eyes were never dry of tears, and his sweet life was ebbing away, as he longed mournfully for his return (*noston oduromenô*).' (v.152–3) Thus Calypso finds him as, having been told by Hermes that the gods have decreed that she should release her unwilling captive, she goes in search of him on the island. Having told him he is now free to go she takes him back to her cave, where Hermes is waiting, and tries to persuade him to stay for one last time:

If in thy heart thou knewest all the measure of woe it is thy fate to fulfil before thou comest to thy native land thou wouldest abide here and keep house with me, and wouldest be immortal, for all thy desire to see thy wife for whom thou longest day by day. Surely not inferior to her do I declare myself to be either in form or stature, for in no wise is it seemly that mortal women should vie with immortals in form or comeliness. (206–13)

Odysseus, answering her, explains to her and to us the reasons for his unhappiness:

Mighty goddess, be not wroth with me for this. I know full

---

7   I use the Loeb translation by A.T. Murray because, to my mind, its slightly old-fashioned feel better represents the quality of the Greek.

well of myself that wise Penelope is meaner to look upon than thou in comeliness and in stature, for she is a mortal, while thou art immortal and ageless. But even so I wish and long day by day to reach my home, and to see the day of my return (*oikade t'elthemenai, kai nostimon êmar idesthai*). (215–20)

Nostos, return, and *oikos*, house, home, come together here, as *nostos* and *gunaikos*, wife, had in the opening lines of the poem. Beautiful and immortal as the nymph is, for Odysseus she is no substitute for his wife, Penelope. Nor is her promise of immortality a sufficient inducement. He knows that by the time he returns both he and Penelope will have aged considerably, whereas Calypso will remain radiant and beautiful for ever, but that, far from holding him back, makes him long for Penelope all the more.

This is because his longing is for more than the familiar beloved figure. It is for his *oikos*, his home, and, as Barbara Cassin notes in her illuminating essay on the concept of nostalgia or the longing for return, to come home does not so much mean to come to a specific place as to come to a place where you are *recognised*.[8] On his travels Odysseus listens to a bard at a local court singing of the exploits of the heroes who fought at Troy and weeps when his own story is sung, and he stiffens when the sirens call him by name to entice him to them. But it is only when he gets to his own island of Ithaca that he is recognised not as a hero of legend but as himself, first by his son, Telemachus, then by his old dog Argos, who looks up, recognises him, wags his tail, and then expires; then by his nurse as she washes the stranger and notes his tell-tale scar; and finally by his wife.

Now past and present can be drawn into conjunction and he can feel that he is himself once more. The years with

---

8   Barbara Cassin, *La Nostalgie: Quand donc est-on chez soi?* (Paris; 2013).

Calypso were a beautiful dream, but for the human being, embodied as we are, a dream, no matter how beautiful, is not enough; immortality, no matter how tempting, a lure. We need to be recognised. We need to return home. The horror of Alzheimer's, the horror of the case histories Sacks relates in *Awakenings*, stems from the fact that the victims are, though alive, no longer at home.

And yet, though Ulysses' homecoming forms the climax of the poem, the point towards which it has been straining since those opening words, and though the poem ends with Odysseus home again, the suitors who have been infecting his house ruthlessly killed, that is not the end for Odysseus. In the great scene in which he reveals himself to his beloved wife and they talk through the night he informs her that, having finally returned, he cannot stay. On his travels he has encountered the seer Tiresias, who prophecied to him, and he repeats more or less word for word what the blind seer said:

> Tiresias bade me go forth to full many cities of men, bearing a shapely oar in my hands, till I should come to men who know naught of the sea, and eat not of food mingled with salt; aye and they know naught of ships... or of shapely oars that serve as wings to ships. And he told me this sign, right manifest; nor will I hide it from thee. When another wayfarer, on meeting me, should say that I had a winnowing fan on my stout shoulder, then he bade me fix my oar in the earth, and make goodly offerings to lord Poseidon – a ram and a bull and a boar... – and depart for my home, and offer sacred hecatombs to the immortal gods, who hold broad heaven, to each one in due order. And death shall come to me myself from the sea, a death so gentle, that shall lay me low, when I am overcome with sleek old age, and my people shall dwell in prosperity around me. All this, he said, should I see fulfilled. (xxiii. 267–84)

This mysterious prophecy and all it entails is accepted without question by Odysseus and by Penelope. It seems that Poseidon, lord of the sea, has to be propitiated, for unless this is done the future prosperity of the islanders of Ithaca will always be in jeopardy. What this entails is going inland so far from the sea that an oar is mistaken by the locals for a winnowing fan, since clearly they have never seen one nor had dealings with men who have, since they eat their food unsalted. There he must sacrifice, presumably to establish the presence even here of the lord of the sea, and, when he has done so, to return home (*oikade aposteichein*). Only then will he be able to die in peace, 'overcome with sleek old age' and knowing that his people 'shall dwell in prosperity around me'.

But even here the mysteries abound. The Greek says that death will come to Odysseus *ex halos*. This is rendered by the Loeb translator, A.T. Murray, as 'far from the sea'. But what does that mean? Nowhere in Ithaca is far from the sea, so perhaps it just means he will die in his bed and not at sea. But others have taken it to mean that death will come to him emerging *out of the sea*, perhaps like a more benign version of the bull who emerges from the waves to destroy Hippolytus in Euripides' play. There is no way for us to reach a decision, one way or the other. And it is entirely appropriate, it seems to me, that this should be so. Odysseus has returned, returned to his home and to his wife, and so, in a sense, to himself. But it is in keeping with Homer's wise realism that this too is seen as provisional. We long to return, we long to be recognised, and we are horrified when we see someone in our midst, someone we know and perhaps love, who does not recognise us or themselves. But that threatens to mythicise return and recognition and to suggest that all of us who do not suffer from a disease that robs us of our past are truly at home. The wise openness of Homer's ending is a gentle reminder of that danger.

II

ONLY HE WHO FORGETS REMEMBERS

Emerson's remark that memory holds together past and present, that it is that which makes the notion of the self possible at all and which 'holds us to our family and friends', would seem to be upheld by Sacks's extraordinary book. But it is badly in need of qualification. Proust for one, barely half a century after Emerson, gives a rather different picture of memory in *À la recherche du temps perdu*. For the whole of that enormous novel is predicated, as Beckett memorably put it in his little book on Proust, on the axiom that 'only he who forgets remembers'.[9]

What does that gnomic phrase mean? Proust seeks to show, in the course of his novel, that there are two sorts of memory, not one. There is our memory of facts and figures, a memory we can set to work, with more or less success, to retrieve events in our immediate and distant past, and then there is involuntary memory, the memory of that which had lain dormant for long periods but which may be activated at any time by a sound, a taste, an unexpected movement. This is because, unlike the other, it is a bodily memory, a memory lodged 'in' our bodies in some mysterious fashion. Thus the chance taste of the 'petite madeleine' many years later suddenly brings flooding

---

9   At least that's how I remembered it. On checking, I have found only this: 'The man with a good memory does not remember anything because he does not forget anything.' (Samuel Beckett, *Proust*, London, 1965, p.29). This must be the only occasion, then, when I find myself writing more pithily than the master of pith.

back into Marcel's body, and then into his mind, the whole lost world of his childhood in Combray. Of course he could, if asked at any time in his subsequent life, have recounted to his interlocutor the facts of his childhood: the summers spent in Combray with great-aunts, the walks, the visitors to the house. But now he suddenly *feels* it all again, he *lives* it all again, and it is this which drives him to try and write down that feeling, to convey to others what he experienced as a child. Later in the novel, bending down to unbutton his boots brings the feel of his long-dead grandmother flooding back. Since her death, he tells us, he had often thought of her, but those thoughts and memories had not really touched him. Now, quite suddenly and unexpectedly, she is as present to him as she was when she was alive. More so, in fact, for when she was alive he had taken her for granted, been busy with his own life, often resented her calls on his attention, whereas now, out of the blue, he finds himself overwhelmed by the sense of what she had always been for him. Thus, feeling her resurrected, as it were, by a chance movement, he also, in practically the same moment, feels the terrible, the unbearable pain of her loss, a pain he had never felt when she died: only he who forgets remembers.

At the same time as Proust brings involuntary memory to our attention he shows that what ordinarily passes for memory tends to be the product only of habit and mental laziness. For what ordinary memory does is to turn what was a confused, often painful and fragmentary set of feelings about what once happened into a narrative, a narrative necessarily constructed according to the conventions of the day. Such a narrative is designed precisely to free us from suffering and confusion, but at the cost of the truth and thus, in the long run, to the detriment of our ability to develop. Thus Swann's 'memory' of his affair with Odette, the anguished peripeties of which we have been following over two hundred pages, in the end consists simply of the cliché: 'To think that I've wasted years of my life... for a woman who didn't appeal to me and who wasn't even my type.'

Sacks, borrowing the term from his mentor, the great Russian neurologist A.R. Luria, often spoke of *proprioception*, that sixth sense we have, the sense of our own bodies which we carry with us from birth to death. It is such an intimate part of ourselves that it tends to be taken for granted, unlike the senses of touch, taste, smell, hearing and sight. It is only when we lose it that we realise that without it we are, in a deep sense, no longer ourselves – which is not true of any of the other senses. Thus a disciple of Sacks, the neurologist Jonathan Cole, recounts the case of a young man who, in the aftermath of gastric flu, lost all sense of his body below his neck and had, by dint of will power and with Cole's help, to be 'taught' how to function again, how to lift a cup to his lips without sending the contents flying over his shoulder, how to raise one foot ever so slightly above the other when negotiating a gently rising path, and so on. One day, alone in the lift, the lights suddenly failed. He was eventually found lying in a heap on the floor: without the ability to see himself he was simply 'not there'.[10] Proust's involuntary memory is clearly linked to proprioception in ways both neurologists and literary critics need to explore.

---

10   Jonathan Cole, *Pride and a Daily Marathon* (London; 1991). There is a delightful essay by John Updike, 'Drinking from a Cup Made Cinchy', a take-off of golfing manuals, which explains how one is to drink a cup of tea and not send the contents shooting over one's shoulder, bringing out the absurdity of trying in words to teach people how to swing a golf club, but which has the effect of making one realise how complicated are those actions which most of us take for granted. This is just what Cole's book does. Updike's essay was first published in *The New Yorker* in 1959.

*

There are further difficulties with the seemingly common-sense view that memory is what holds the self together and that therefore the loss of memory means the loss of self. In his story 'Funes the Memorious' Borges writes of a man who can forget nothing:

> Locke in the seventeenth century postulated (and rejected) an impossible language in which each individual thing, each stone, each bird and each branch, would have its own name. Funes once projected an analogous language but discarded it because it seemed too general to him, too ambiguous. Funes remembered not only every tree of every wood but also every one of the times he had perceived or imagined it.

However, far from this extraordinary visual memory giving Funes a huge advantage over the rest of us, it makes him, to all intents and purposes incapable of thought and quite unable to live a normal life:

> Not only was it difficult for him to comprehend that the general symbol dog embraces so many unlike individuals of diverse size and form, it bothered him that the dog at three fourteen (seen from the side) should have the same name as the dog at three fifteen (seen from the front). His own face in the mirror, his own hands, surprised him every time he saw them... It was very difficult for him to sleep.

Funes in the end remains confined to his room and dies shortly after the narrator has encountered him.

What the case of Funes brings out is that what we call 'memory' is in fact a highly selective mechanism and that someone with the prefect memory of a Funes is a monster, totally unable to function in the real world. Plato may not have been correct in thinking that all dogs derive from the perfect Idea of a dog laid up in heaven but, as always, he put his finger on a philosophical puzzle, which is that language is powerfully abstractive and that it is to this that it owes its success. We say: 'This is a dog, this is a tree', and other people understand us even if they see far more differences between individual dogs and trees than we do (if they are dog breeders, say, or botanists). It is also true that many artists and writers since the time of the Romantics have felt frustrated by this and have felt the need (as Borges does here) to alert us not just to the variety but to the *thisness* of the world around us, the mystery of it as it is, to make us 'see the earth again/ Cleared of its stiff and stubborn, man-locked set', as Wallace Stevens put it in his beautiful late poem, 'Angel Surrounded by Paysans'. One thinks of Roquentin's nausea at seeing the root of a tree as if for the first time, unshackled from the words for 'root of a tree' in Sartre's *Nausea*; of Hopkins' rapture at catching sight of (and catching in his poetry the feel of) a kingfisher suddenly taking off; of the entire life-project of a Monet or a Cézanne to see the world not as we think of it but as it is at the moment the artist engages with it. Valéry, in one of his essays on Degas, speaks with admiration of how the painter would throw a bunched handkerchief or a piece of coal onto the table and then try to draw it – this particular handkerchief, fallen in this particular unique way, this particular lump of coal, broken in this particular unique way. The examples could be multiplied.

*

I doubt if Borges knew the work of Luria, who was active in Russia in the first half of the twentieth century and whose books were brought to the attention of a wider public by Sacks in the seventies and eighties. Yet one of Luria's most famous case studies concerns a man who suffers – that has to be the right word – from the same condition as Borges' imaginary youth. In *The Mind of a Mnemonist* (the book was completed in 1965 and came out in the US in 1967 and in Britain the following year) Luria examines the strange case of S., a Jewish Moscow journalist who, when he came to him, could remember everything but make sense of very little. For example, it was difficult for him to remember people he had previously met because he could not abstract from the moment of perception. 'People's faces are constantly changing,' he told Luria. 'It's the different shades of expression that confuse me and make it so hard for me to remember faces.'

S.'s mind was stocked with vivid images. Each word he heard or read brought with it a graphic image:

> When I hear the word *green*, a green flowerpot appears, with the word *red* I see a man in a red shirt coming towards me; as for *blue* this means an image of someone waving a small blue flag from a window… Even numbers remind me of images. Take the number 1. This is a well-built man; 2 is a high-spirited woman; 3 is a gloomy person (why I don't know);… 8 is a very stout woman, a sack within a sack…

Luria explains how when S. became a professional mnemonist he refined this innate gift or curse in the following way:

> When S. read through a long list of words, each word would elicit a graphic image. And since the series was fairly long he had to find some way of distributing these images of his in a mental row or sequence. Most often… he would 'distribute' them along some roadway or street he visualized in his mind. Sometimes this was a street in his home town which would also include the yard attached to the house he had lived in as a child, which he recalled

vividly. On the other hand, he might also select a street in Moscow. Frequently he would take a mental walk along that street – Gorky Street in Moscow, beginning at Mayakovsky Square – and slowly make his way down, 'distributing' his images at houses, gates and store windows.[11]

If he was asked to give the word preceding or following a word picked at random from a sequence, 'he would simply begin his walk, either from the beginning or end of the street, find the image of the object I had named, and "take a look at" whatever happened to be situated on either side of it.' (31)

What S. didn't seem to know (and Luria does not mention it either) was that this was the time-honoured method of memorising, going back to classical antiquity. That history has been mapped by Frances Yates in her groundbreaking book, *The Art of Memory* (1966), and explored in some depth by her students and followers in the subsequent decades. S's case, though, was very different from that of those trained for a lifetime of oratory or the compilation of books in the ancient and medieval worlds, in that the intensity of his visual imagination and his natural habit of converting everything he read or heard into vivid images actually made ordinary life extremely difficult for him. There was, as we have seen, the problem of people and faces, but even worse was the processing of information, which for most of us is so easy that we are not even aware of it. Here is his own account:

I was read a phrase: 'B was leaning up against a tree...' I saw a slim young man dressed in a dark blue suit (...). He was standing near a big linden tree with grass and woods all around... But then the sentence went on: 'and was peering into a shop window'. Now how do you like that? It means the scene isn't set in the woods, or

---

11   A.R. Luria, *The Mind of the Mnemonist* (London; 1968), pp.30–1.

in a garden, but he's standing on a street. And I have to start the whole sentence over from the beginning... (87)

Far from helping him to remember, in his ordinary dealings with the world images proved an obstacle to understanding, preventing S. from concentrating on the essential. 'Moreover,' comments Luria, 'since these tended to jam together, producing more images, he was carried so far adrift that he was forced to go back and rethink the entire passage. Consequently, understanding a simple passage – a phrase for that matter – would turn out to be a Sisyphean task.'

Thus, while most of us would be delighted if we could find ways to improve our memories, in S.'s case the reverse was true. In order to make life bearable he needed to be able to forget. Plato had worried that the invention of writing would lead to the atrophy of memory, and he was of course partly right. S., on the other hand, tried to write things down so as to *free himself from the need to remember them.* 'But I got nowhere,' he confessed to Luria. 'For in my mind I continued to see what I'd written.' He even tried burning what he'd written, but that didn't work either for in his imagination he still saw every detail of every page he had burned.'

*

As we have got to know more about what it is that makes us, human beings, function as we do, we have discovered that the simple binaries with which it is conventional to operate – being sighted and being blind, being able to hear and being deaf, having a memory and losing one's memory, being mad or being sane – these binaries do not really exist. Instead there is a continuum of experience between very good sight and total blindness, very good hearing and total deafness, and so on. The brain, we have learned, is a powerfully abstracting as well as a powerfully concretising force. And we are also coming to understand the large part learning and the expectations of society play in whatever we think of as purely natural experiences. Moreover, the child constructs the world in its first months and years, the world is not simply revealed to it. It learns to distinguish sights and sounds, to speak and understand what others are saying, to remember even and forget, all in the interests of acculturation, of entering the world of what Freud called 'civilisation and its discontents', the world of the trade-offs we constantly have to make between immediate gratification and long-term satisfaction. We live our lives, for the most part, blissfully unaware of all this – until something goes wrong and we realise what we have lost.

III
'REMEMBER KOSOVO!'
'REMEMBER AUSCHWITZ!'

It is not only in the private realm that today we are terrified of forgetting. How many times since the end of the Second World War have we heard the cry: 'We must not forget!', and, hearing it, repeated it in our hearts. In the face of the rising tide of xenophobia once again sweeping across Europe and the United States, in the face of growing anti-Semitism and Islamophobia, in the face of the ignorance of those born long after the war, it has seemed obvious that every effort must be made to ensure that the atrocities committed by the Nazis and their accomplices should not disappear from memory.

And it is not only today, seventy years and more after the liberation of the Camps, that the injunction not to forget appears particularly forceful. It was there in the hearts and on the lips of those who suffered precisely because one of the imperatives of the Nazis was to eradicate the memory of what they had done. They failed, but their failure only makes us conscious of the fact that they might have succeeded. The eradication of memory was their aim, and not just in self-protection but also as part and parcel of their determination to eradicate a whole people whose survival has in the past always been particularly dependent on memory, since, being without a land, it was only memory that preserved their sense of themselves as a people. The Nazi crime was a crime against countless individuals, but it was also a crime against a people who had, at the centre of their affective being, the injunction *zakhor*, remember – remember what God did to Israel, how

He saved it from annihilation in Egypt and then made it a great nation, remember at every Passover that had *they* not been saved then *we* would not be here, now. The question of memory, then, when dealing with this episode in European history, is not peripheral but absolutely central.

And yet, as with individual memory, as soon as one examines it the matter ceases to seem so clear-cut. For what does the injunction not to forget really mean? How many of us have personal memories of those events? In fifty years' time the question will not even make sense any more. How can we ask people not to forget what they have never known? Is not the word *forget* perhaps the wrong one? Perhaps what we mean is that people should know the history of Europe in the twentieth century well enough to deal with the rise of new forms of discrimination and violence against minorities and to refute those who deny that these events ever happened or that if they happened they were nothing like as bad as 'people' try to make out.

But that is not quite right. It is too cold, too cerebral. No doubt a better-informed public is desirable, no doubt events such as Holocaust Memorial Day, with its large educational component, is valuable and important. But when politicians and others proclaim the mantra 'We must not forget!' they are thinking of something far more immediate, far more visceral, than simply the need for better schooling. But that is the problem. Uttering such slogans puts us in company we would prefer not to keep, the company of the likes of Milošević and Karadžić in the Yugoslav civil wars of the nineties and of extremist Irish Catholics and Protestants during the Troubles. For it is striking how often we hear that cry from the lips of those we regard as dangerous demagogues, people who seem to be locked into a world of fantasy and delusion, though in their own eyes they are of course utterly righteous. Coming from Serb and Irish leaders in the nineties the slogan seemed to be denying others the right to argue with them, a fanning of the flames of bigotry, fanaticism and self-pity. 'Remember Kosovo!' 'Remember Bloody Sunday!' we used to hear – and what is the difference between these calls to memory and the cry: 'Remember Auschwitz!' 'Remember the Camps!'?

One immediate difference would seem to be that one is a call to action and the other is not. But that is not quite right either. Anyone with an interest in the Middle East and in the fate of Israel among its Arab neighbours will recall the way in which Begin and the Israeli right have used the injunction not to forget the Holocaust as a way of justifying aggression and warding off the moral indignation of the world at the Israeli treatment of the Palestinians. And Netanyahu is still at it. There is no difference between the injunction to remember Kosovo trumpeted by Serb nationalists in the 1990s and the injunction to remember Auschwitz trumpeted by Begin and Netanyahu. In both cases the implicit 'never again!' is used to reinforce what the great Jewish historian of the Jews, Salo Baron, called the lachrymose version of Jewish history ('Look how we suffered at their hands!') and to justify actions which are morally reprehensible and legally suspect.

But, it will be argued, they have simply hijacked for their own ends perfectly respectable, indeed highly desirable attitudes. Surely what they have done with the injunction not to forget has nothing to do with what millions of people, Jews and non-Jews, have felt since the full extent of the Nazi atrocities came to light seventy-five years ago: namely, that these things were so appalling that we need to keep them constantly before us if we are to make sure they are never repeated. That is perfectly true and, as I suggested at the outset of this chapter, it is a view no right-thinking person could fail to share. Yet I don't think we can separate it quite so easily from the views of Serbian and Irish leaders in the 1990s, or of their Israeli counterparts then and today.

In the tangled politics of the Middle East Israeli leaders are not the only ones who have played the memory game. In his powerful polemic against the injunction not to forget, *In Praise of Forgetting*, David Rieff points to the example of the modern use of the word 'crusade' by Arab leaders. He cites the distinguished historian of memory, Paul Connerton: 'Medieval Muslim historians did not share with the medieval European Christians the sense of witnessing a great struggle between Islam and Christendom for the control of the Holy Land.' The medieval Arab chroniclers never used the word 'crusade' or 'crusader', for example, but rather 'Franks' and 'infidels'. But beginning some time in the nineteenth century, writes Rieff, 'an expanding body of Arabic historical writing has taken the Crusades as its theme, with the term gradually taking on the connotations of 'a code word for the malign intentions of the Western powers… culminating in the foundation of the State of Israel'. By the 1980s the link between the Kingdom of Jerusalem (established in the First Crusade in 1099) and the modern state of Israel had come to seem so self-evident to many Arab artists and intellectuals that the Palestinian poet Mahmoud Darwish could write of the 1982 Israeli siege of Beirut as being the work of 'left-over Crusaders taking their revenge for all medieval history.'[12]

Darwish, like Begin, is not totally wrong. And we might even argue that, like Eliot and Joyce and especially David Jones in his great poem about World War I, *In Parenthesis*, he is merely working in a poetic vein that seeks to give meaning to contemporary events by bringing out their parallels to ancient myths and bygone times. The trouble with this is that the grain of truth in Darwish's appropriation of the term simplifies what is complex and so makes any attempt to move

12   David Rieff, *In Praise of Forgetting: Historical Memory and Its Ironies* (London; 2016), p.132.

forward politically or even in terms of understanding, even more difficult. There were several reasons why the Crusaders undertook the arduous journey to Jerusalem. The main one was of course religious zeal, but mixed with it there was no doubt the desire for loot and the wish on the part of many to seek glory and adventure in far-off places. There were likewise many reasons for the founding of the State of Israel – idealism and the desire to get away from the stifling atmosphere of the East European shtetl on the part of the early settlers, religious zeal on the part of a small minority, and above all the overwhelming need to provide a national home for the Jewish people, made all the more pressing by the almost total annihilation of European Jewry in World War II. None of this is addressed by calling the Israelis 'left-over Crusaders... taking their revenge for all medieval history'. And that is the problem with public memory. As Rieff says, 'the takeover of history by memory is also the takeover of history by politics' (63).

Politics founded on myth and simplification, on a binary opposition between black and white, bad and good, perpetrators and victims is a dangerous game that nearly always ends badly.

David Rieff draws attention in his book, *In Praise of Forgetting,*
to the Edict of Nantes, drawn up by Henry IV at the end of
the sixteenth century French wars of religion, which, among
other things, decrees that: 'The memory of all things that took
place on one side or the other from March 1585... and in
all of the preceding troubles, will remain extinguished and
treated as something that did not take place.' (143) Such an
attempt to impose forgetting by fiat surely remains a unique
experiment. However, as with Ireland and the Good Friday
Agreement, the longer peace holds, however often broken by
sporadic violence and accusations and counter-accusations,
the better the chance that the past and its animosities can
come to seem less pressing as new realities emerge. The past
cannot and perhaps should not be buried, but it can fade into
irrelevance – though one can never take that for granted, for
as we will see with statues in public places, it is always liable to
be awoken by ruthless demagogues.

Nelson Mandela is of course the name always evoked in this
context, and he is certainly one of the clearest modern examples
of a statesman who used his authority to shape a narrative
of his country that refused to put the remembering of past
wrongs at the centre of the story. But his story is in some ways
too pure, too clean. A more challenging example of a modern
statesman who recognised the value of burying the past is
Charles de Gaulle, just because his interventions were never
clearly right. In August 1944, when he made his triumphal
entry into Paris at the head of the Free French army, he was

determined that France should not tear itself apart as those who had collaborated with Vichy and the Germans sought to minimise their involvement and those who had resisted sensed that their hour had come. A few major figures of the Vichy regime were tried and in some cases executed, but that was it. For thirty years the myth of the glorious French Resistance (but always seen as an arm of de Gaulle's Free French army, with the Communists airbrushed) was carefully fostered and many of the old collaborators such as the infamous Maurice Papon were even given quite senior positions in successive French governments. Marcel Ophuls' searing documentary about the war in the Clermond-Ferrand area, *Le Chagrin et la pitié* (*The Sorrow and the Pity*), with its even-handed depiction of both collaboration and resistance, which was made in 1969, was at first banned from French television; though shown by the BBC, it was not aired in France till 1982. And it was only in the 1990s that Papon, who had been responsible for the murder of 1600 Jews during the war and was implicated, among other crimes, in the murder of the Algerian leader Ben Barka in 1962, was finally brought to trial and convicted of Crimes Against Humanity. Barely two months after taking office in 1995, President Chirac publicly recognized France's responsibility for deporting thousands of Jews to Nazi death camps during the German occupation in World War II. 'These dark hours forever sully our history and are an insult to our past and our traditions,' he said during ceremonies marking the fifty-third anniversary of the first mass arrests of Jews in Paris. 'Yes, the criminal folly of the occupiers was seconded by the French, by the French state.' And he went on: 'France, the homeland of the Enlightenment and of the rights of man, a land of welcome and asylum, on that day committed the irreparable. Breaking its word, it handed those who were under its protection over to their executioners.' He concluded by saying of the victims: 'We owe them an everlasting debt.'

In the wake of Ophuls' film it became fashionable in liberal circles to accuse de Gaulle and successive French governments of fostering the myth of the heroic French nation resisting the Occupation at the expense of historical truth. But though this was of course true it failed to reckon with the difficult choices statesmen have to make, and the greater the statesman the more difficult the choices he is prepared to confront. De Gaulle of course had his own myth of the greatness of France, of which he had, he felt, become the custodian, just as Churchill had his of Britain's. This is what made them such inspiring war-time leaders. But he must have known that the truth was quite otherwise, that, as with every nation, there were in France in those years some heroes, some who acted despicably and a great many who kept their heads down and waited to see which way the wind would blow. But as the undisputed voice of France at the end of the war he felt that it was more important, for the long-term well-being of the nation, to brush some things under the carpet and allow them to emerge only when emotions were less raw, rather than feel righteous and insist that France not forget anything that had happened. And this seems to have been a persistent and conscious practice of his. When, in the early 1960s, he made the momentous decision that France would have to accede to Algerian independence, the story goes, one of his advisers protested: 'So much blood has been shed. Was that all for nothing?' To which de Gaulle replied: '*Rien ne seche plus vite que le sang.*' Nothing dries quicker than blood.

*

No one can know for sure whether de Gaulle was a wise statesman or a man so obsessed with his own vision of France that he set understanding of what really happened back by more than a quarter of a century. What can be said for certain though is that the modern mantra that only full disclosure will bring closure is itself as much of a myth as that of the entire French nation united in its resistance to the Nazis. Its roots lie deep in Protestant culture (and in the Protestant strain in Catholic culture which goes back to St Augustine), with its notion that the road to salvation will only be revealed when we have recognised our sins and laid them before the all-merciful God. That this kind of thinking lies behind even such a seemingly secular modern discipline as psychoanalysis only shows how deeply Protestant thinking penetrated Western culture in the course of the past four centuries.

Take one of the most celebrated documentary films of recent years, Claude Lanzmann's *Shoah*. Lanzmann, a former Resistance fighter and then editor with Sartre and Simone de Beauvoir of *Les Temps Modernes*, spent eleven years making the film, which runs to over ten hours. Eschewing archival material, he concentrates on interviews with three groups of witnesses to the Holocaust: survivors, bystanders and perpetrators. But these are no ordinary interviews. We watch Lanzmann attempting to prize out the memories of a series of mainly reluctant interviewees. Historians have heaped praise on the film and routinely use it in seminars and lectures on the Holocaust. But I for one find it almost unwatchable, not because it deals with unimaginable horrors (after all, by now anyone at all concerned with the subject is largely familiar with this), but because, especially where the victims of the Nazis are concerned, as with the barber he interviews in an early episode, it shows us a powerful, articulate and authoritative man browbeating his subjects, forcing them to speak about things they seem desperate not to (and yet they must, presumably, have offered to take part).

Lanzmann's film takes the attitude that to remember and speak out one's memories can only be good. In this it belongs, like many of Hitchcock's films where the same maxim is taken for granted, firmly in the Freudian century, the century, that is, of the banalisation of Freud's ideas, a central pillar of which is that what is not said is being repressed and that it can only be good for the patient and for society as a whole that the repressed should be released to emerge into the light of day. Leaving aside the question of whether this is what the mature Freud advocated, let us ask another: is it true?

There is a word which once had great prestige in English culture but which has, in recent times, fallen into abeyance. That word is *reticence*, with its adjective, *reticent*. It derives from the Latin *re*, again, + *tacere*, to be silent. The OED dates the noun to 1603 and gives a series of interrelated meanings: 'Maintenance of silence; avoidance of speaking freely; disposition to say little.' It rather surprisingly dates the adjective to 1834 and gives roughly parallel but subtly different sets of meanings for it: 'Reserved; disinclined to speak freely; given to silence or concealment.' This is extraordinarily confused, for it takes but a little thought to see that 'disposition to say little' and 'disinclined to speak freely' are very different things, as are 'given to silence' and 'given to concealment'. The first definition describes a type of character, someone we would call self-contained or, more negatively, taciturn; the second describes what might be a character trait but seems more likely to be the result of a situation, one in which it is felt necessary to conceal something or to avoid saying something for one's own advantage or for fear of the consequences, real or imaginary. The first set describes someone we all feel we could admire, a person who does not shoot his mouth off at all times, who weighs his words. The second describes someone who has or thinks he has something to hide, and is thus inherently suspicious. It does not take much imagination to see that when the first kind of person is no longer understood he starts to be described in terms of the second: my quiet and self-contained person becomes your suspicious character, someone hiding a secret, someone who, you may feel, needs to be made to talk.

In 1548 while still a teenager, the future Queen Elizabeth wrote to her brother, King Edward VI: 'It is (as your majesty is not unaware) rather characteristic of my nature not only not to say in words as much as I think in my mind, but also, indeed, not to say more than I think. This latter of which (I mean saying more), as few defend it, so many use it everywhere, but mostly indeed in the courts of princes and kings...' The future queen is clearly proud of her never saying more than she thinks. The opposite to this, flattery and hypocrisy, are clearly condemned, though Elizabeth is realistic enough to recognise that it naturally exists, and nowhere more so than at court.

And, of course, it is in a king's court that Shakespeare sets his most spectacular dramatisation of what the young Elisabeth was talking about: Cordelia's refusal to play the game of her older sisters by telling their father, King Lear, not the truth, but what he wants to hear. 'Speak,' says Lear to her when her sisters have spoken. To which she answers, 'Nothing, my lord.'

> Nothing?
> Nothing.
> Nothing will come of nothing: speak again.
> Unhappy that I am, I cannot heave
> My heart into my mouth: I love your Majesty
> According to my bond; no more, no less. (I.i.86–93)

But this striking scene is perhaps too fairy-tale-like for our purposes. The issue, after all, is not one of honesty versus flattery but of trying to separate reticence from concealment. And for that another Shakespeare play is perhaps more helpful in bringing to our attention not only an older way of thinking about the self, but also how that older way was starting to come under fire. I am talking of course about *Hamlet*, the first Quarto of which was published in 1603 (the date the OED gives for the first appearance of the word *reticence*), though scholars think the play was probably written a year or two before.

The notion of silence as concealment lies heavy upon the world of the court at Elsinore, where everyone is trying to conceal something from everyone else, where spies are everywhere and where rumour and counter-rumour spread like wildfire. In the midst of all this stands Hamlet himself, and his very presence, his gnomic and wittily cutting remarks, his dignity and uprightness, are a living rebuke to the Danish court's version of human character. Nowhere is this brought out more clearly than in the scene with his old schoolmates Rosencrantz and Guildenstern, now firmly in the camp of Claudius, where Hamlet wittily attempts to show them not just that he knows very well what they are up to, but that the court's premise that there is a truth hidden inside a person which a little probing can coax into the open is based on a false understanding of what constitutes human nature.

Before the entry of the two courtiers Hamlet has called for recorders, those simple woodwind instruments every beginner is expected to master, to be brought out. Now they are handed to him just in time for him to use them to give his old friends a little lesson on the nature of man. Why, he begins by asking them, using a hunting image, 'do you go about to recover the wind of me' (so that I can pick up your scent and run away from you and straight into a trap)? Oh my lord, responds Guildenstern, feigning innocence, we have only come because we are so fond of you. Hamlet affects puzzlement and seemingly switches topic:

> Will you play upon the pipes?
> My lord, I cannot.
> I pray you.
> Believe me, I cannot.
> I do beseech you.

I have no touch of it, my lord.

It is as easy as lying. Govern these ventages with your fingers and thumb, give it breath with your mouth, and it will discourse most eloquent music. Look you, these are the stops.

But these I cannot command to any utterance of harmony. I have not the skill.

Why, look you now, how unworthy a thing you make of me. You would play upon me, you would seem to know my stops, you would pluck the heart out of my mystery, you would sound me from my lowest to the top of my compass; and there is much music, excellent voice, in this little organ, yet cannot you make it speak. 'Sblood, do you think I am easier to be played upon than a pipe? Call me what instrument you will, though you fret me, you cannot play upon me. (B text, III.ii.341–63, Arden 3rd series)

The last line has Hamlet switching from a wind to a stringed instrument, equipped with frets, the ridges which mark the place for the fingers – but 'to fret' also means of course to irritate (today it mainly means to feel irritable). The whole little scene is Hamlet's exposition of what he sees as man's nature, first in the form of an impersonal demonstration but then bursting out into his true feelings at the end. Man, he is saying, is not a machine which you can open up and whose interior you can inspect; he is more like a musical instrument, which must be coaxed into giving voice by those who know how to play, in a kind of collaborative endeavour (we have seen Sacks making a similar point in his argument with the mid-twentieth century medical profession). Man is of course infinitely more complex than a simple recorder, yet Rosencrantz, who cannot even play the recorder, imagines that he can play upon a human being and make him speak 'his soul'. 'Call me what instrument you will,' Hamlet laughingly tells the two courtiers, 'even though you try to play upon me, all you do is irritate me and you certainly cannot make me speak.'

Of course things are more complicated than that in this rich and complicated play. Hamlet *does* of course have something to hide, namely the fact that he has seen his father's ghost and has received from him the injunction to avenge him. But just as he cannot go along with the courtiers' view of what constitutes human beings, so he cannot (quite) go along with his father's view of what has to be done. He feels himself to be stranded in an intellectual and imaginative no-man's land. He has arrived too late in the day to be able to accept the simple revenge code to which his father (and Laertes) subscribe, but too early, perhaps, to accept the court's view of how life should be lived. And despite his words to Rosencrantz and Guildenstern, he is just as prone as they are to want to look inside himself to see what is there, to determine what it is he *really* feels, *really* believes. What the play shows us is that this is to ask the wrong question even when it is Hamlet doing the asking, or perhaps that to ask such a question at all is already to be on the wrong track. For, like everyone in the play, Hamlet does but scantly know himself, and he dies still not having understood. What we as spectators are made to grasp, though, by the way Shakespeare has constructed his play, is that while a person is not just a machine, he is not a single thing either. Rather, he is the sum of his actions and his words. Thus what a person truly 'is' can never be grasped by that person, for it only becomes visible after their death, that event which, as Mallarmé put it in his sonnet in memory of Edgar Allen Poe, changes us for ever into who we are – *tel qu'en lui-même l'éternité le change.*

So many of Shakespeare's works, but the great tragedies in particular, are concerned with the transition from medieval to modern, from an older culture and view of man to the one we take for granted today. But talk of transition hides the fact that we still partly live in both worlds and that it is a diminution of our potential to see ourselves only through the prism of the modern. We need to keep those older meanings alive: by reading Homer the older meanings of native land; by reading Aeschylus' *Oresteia* the older meanings of *oikos* or house; by reading *Hamlet* the older meanings of reticence. Hamlet does not speak or only speaks in riddles not so much because he has something to hide as because he has something to say for which he cannot find the words. To elide 'reticence' with 'repression' and 'disposition to say little' with 'avoidance of speaking freely' is to lose something precious in our understanding of ourselves and in our way of conducting ourselves. A survivor's right to say little should not be treated as denial but respected for what it is, a tacit recognition that all words are distorting and inadequate to the experience, and a recognition too that 'forgetting' takes many forms, not all of them negative.

The Human Rights barrister, Phillipe Sands' extraordinary book, *East West Street*, is in part a search for what happened to his family in Europe in the war years; in part an attempt to unearth the lives of two remarkable twentieth-century jurists, Hersch Lauterpach, who developed the legal concept of Crimes Against Humanity, and Rafael Lemkin, who developed the legal concept of Genocide, and who, by a strange coincidence, were both natives, like Sands' grandfather, of the (now) Ukrainian town of Lviv; and in part the story of how the two concepts jostled for primacy in international law during the Nuremberg Trials and after. But one of the more memorable scenes concerns none of these important issues but rather a purely private moment. Sands travels to Israel to talk to his grandfather's niece, Herta Gruber, both of whose parents perished in the Holocaust. At the end of a strange conversation, brokered by her son, in which she mainly listens to what Sands has to tell her about what he has discovered about her parents' last days, she suddenly says to him: 'I want you to know that it's not correct that I have forgotten anything... It is just that I decided a long time ago that this was a period I did not wish to remember. I have not forgotten. I have chosen not to remember.'

Wisely, Sands leaves it open how we are to respond to her statement.

V

NIETZSCHE AND THE NEED TO SLEEP

Nietzsche begins the second of his *Untimely Meditations* with a striking, a shocking (though, Nietzsche being Nietzsche, a comic) little scene: 'Consider the cattle grazing as you pass them by,' he writes:

> They do not know what is meant by yesterday or today, they leap about, eat, rest, digest, leap about again, and so from morn till night, and from day to day, fettered to the moment and its pleasure or displeasure, and thus neither melancholy nor bored. This is a hard sight for man to see; for though he thinks himself better than the animals because he is human, he cannot help envying them their happiness – what they have, a life neither bored nor painful, is precisely what he wants, yet he cannot have it because he refuses to be like an animal. A human being may well ask an animal: 'Why do you not speak to me of your happiness, but only stand and gaze at me?' The animal would like to answer and say: 'The reason I always forgot what I was going to say is' – but then he forgot this answer too and stayed silent, so that the human being was left wondering.
>
> But he also wonders at himself that he cannot learn to forget but clings relentlessly to the past: however far and fast he may run this chain runs with him.[13]

---

13   Friedrich Nietzsche, *Untimely Meditations*, tr. J.Hollingdale (Cambridge; 1983), pp.60–1.

As always with Nietzsche it is not so much the answers he gives as the questions he asks that makes him worth reading. What he asks in this essay is, in effect, the simple but devastating question: Why history? He is not so much interested in what history is or what is the best way to do it but simply why we feel we *need* history, why we write it and why we read it. And his answer is not so much an attack on the profession of history as a challenge to us to question what we take for granted in order to show us that it is not natural, not a part of the order of nature, but an acquisition and thus the result of choices both conscious and unconscious, on our part, on the part of mankind.

Nietzsche wrote the *Untimely Meditations* (*Unzeitgemasse Betrachtungen* - *Meditations Against the Times* might be a better way of putting it) between 1873 and 1875, in the immediate aftermath of the Prussian victory over France in 1870 (where he had served as a medical orderly), when Prussian triumphalism and nationalism were at their height. It consists of four long essays, three of them on key figures in mid-century German thought and culture: David Strauss, Arthur Schopenhauer, Richard Wagner. The first scandalised many readers with his critical *Life of Jesus* (translated by George Eliot), the last two were and remained dominant figures in Nietzsche's pantheon, father-figures from whom he struggled to free himself all his life. The fourth essay, the one we are concerned with here, was more general, its tricky German title, 'Vom Nutzen und Nachteil der Historie für das Leben', variously translated as 'On the Use and Abuse of History' and 'On the Advantage and Disadvantage of History for Life'.

The essay actually begins not with the little vignette I have just quoted but with a Forward, which opens with a quote from Nietzsche's great hero, Goethe: 'I hate everything that merely instructs me without augmenting or directly invigorating my activity' (59). And in one of his last books, *The Twilight of the Idols*, he returns to Goethe and to this theme: what he admires in Goethe, he says there, is his 'limited perspectives', his ability to set himself a host of strictly defined and practical goals. Goethe is not, says Nietzsche, one large thing, a 'genius', but rather a man who did many different things supremely well: he wrote novels, poetry and plays, ran a theatre, advised rulers, studied the ways plants grow and how we perceive colours. He never stood still, his enquiring mind and spirit drove him to try and master whatever he took a fancy to, and he never sought to acquire knowledge simply for its own sake but always in order to feed his creativity. Thus he remained alive and open for the whole of his long life. By contrast Nietzsche's contemporaries, he suggests, seem to believe that simply knowing more is an unquestioned good. Wrong, says Nietzsche in book after book. That leads only to leadenness and depression and even to suicidal despair.

His primary target is the school of historians that had grown up round the great mid-century German scholar, Leopold Ranke, whose guiding principle was the notion that the historian, in his famous formulation, should try to show 'what actually happened' by the careful accumulation of facts. We must not be swayed by our emotions, he and his disciples argued, what we have to do is to adopt the same stance in the face of history as the scientist in the face of nature.

Ranke's influence quickly spread beyond his chosen field. Nietzsche confronted it in his role as a young professor of classical philology. 'What is preferred,' he wrote of the attitude prevalent in classical studies as he found them:

is that which produces no emotion at all and where the driest phrase is the right phrase. One goes so far, indeed, as to believe that he to whom a moment of the past means nothing at all is the proper man to describe it. This is frequently the relationship between classicists and the Greeks they study: they mean nothing to one another – a state of affairs called 'objectivity'. (93)

By contrast, as he had already demonstrated in *The Birth of Tragedy* (1872), Nietzsche had become a classicist because he believed the classics had much to teach our very different modern culture – much to teach it precisely because it was so different in its assumptions and in the way it viewed the world. The Germans are in thrall to the ancient Greeks, he says, but only as epigones, as those who come after, who admire from afar, almost as though from another planet. What they must be made to see is that the ancient Greeks, read properly, could invigorate their moribund culture. The full title of the 1872 volume was *The Birth of Tragedy from the Spirit of Music*, and though it deals with Greek tragedy its hidden referent is Richard Wagner, the man Nietzsche believed at the time could bring the spirit of ancient Greek tragedy back to modern Germany.[14]

This relationship to the past, what we might call a living relationship to it, which comes instinctively to Nietzsche and that he advocates in this essay is one that will find echoes in many twentieth century artists. History, for Joyce's alter ego, Stephen Dedalus, was a nightmare from which he was trying to awake, while Stravinsky is recorded by Robert Craft as having said to those who criticised him for plagiarising Pergolesi in *Pulcinella*, 'You "respect", I love.' Eliot, in the magisterial tone he adopted to make his more revolutionary pronouncements, echoes this in his lapidary phrase: 'Bad poets imitate; good poets steal.' The past, they all feel, should be plundered for our needs, not worshipped as a monument.

---

14   In his later writings he spectacularly changed his mind about Wagner, seeing him more as the exemplar of what was worst in the world of the later nineteenth century and setting against the leadenness of his music and the 'backstairs psychology' of his characters, who, he felt, were merely bourgeois Germans dressed up as mythological heroes and heroines.

But of course the Rankean way of doing history is not just deadly for the health of a people, it may not even be a very good way of doing history. Walter Benjamin, in his last great work, 'Theses on the Philosophy of History', is in no doubt of that. 'To articulate the past historically does not mean to recognise it "the way it really was"', he says, explicitly quoting the Rankean phrase. And he goes on:

> Historicism [that is, the Rankean model] contents itself with establishing a causal connection between various moments in history. But no fact that is a cause is for that very reason historical. It becomes historical posthumously, as it were, through events that may be separated from it by thousands of years. A historian who takes this as his point of departure stops telling the sequence of events like the beads of a rosary. Instead he grasps the constellation which his own era has formed with a definite earlier one. Thus he establishes a conception of the present as 'the time of the now', which is shot through with the chips of Messianic time.[15]

Neither Nietzsche nor Stravinsky, Eliot and Benjamin, is advocating the notion that there is no truth, that everything is simply a matter of perspective. It is because Nietzsche was convinced that ancient Greek culture was utterly different from the culture of the modern Germans, that its ideals and premises were totally alien to those of nineteenth-century Europeans, that he wanted them to learn from it. It is, he argues, the advocates of historicism in all its forms who are distorting the truth. By seeing the ancient Greeks (or Donne or Pergolesi) simply as part of a continuum with no other meaning for us today than as figures in an endless chain, they are not seeing them as living presences and therefore not

---

15 Walter Benjamin, *Illuminations* ed. Hannah Arendt, tr. Harry Zohn (London; 1970), p.265.

seeing them at all. There may be disagreement about *what* they were like, but that is natural in the human sciences; what is important is that we recognise what a *living* past may have to offer to the present. And in that spirit Nietzsche tries to bring the past alive for us.

*

As he matured Nietzsche saw more clearly just what was at stake in his critique of the scientific spirit, the spirit of disinterested study, that was becoming the accepted attitude in the humanities as well as in the sciences in his day. 'We whose business it is to inquire have gradually grown suspicious of all believers,' he says in a late work, *The Genealogy of Morals* (1887). And there he presses forward with his insight that even if these scientific spirits believe themselves to be free of all belief they still cherish one belief, the belief that their method is the right one: 'These men are a long way from being *free* spirits, because they still believe in truth.' It is not that he wants to do away with all notion of truth, it is that he does not believe truth to be one thing, Truth, with a capital T, a kind of mountain which will inevitably rise up, whole and majestic, from the myriads of pieces of research being carried out in every conceivable field by all these earnest spirits. 'Nothing could be more foreign to our intransigents than true freedom and detachment; they are securely tied to their belief in truth – more securely than anyone else.' The 'will to truth,' he goes on:

> is the belief in a metaphysical value, in that absolute value of 'the true' which stems from the ascetic ideal and stands or falls with it. Strictly speaking, there is no such thing as a science without assumptions; the very notion of such a science is unthinkable, absurd. A philosophy, a 'faith' is always needed to give science a direction, a meaning, a limit, a *raison d'être*... It appears that today

inquiry itself stands in need of justification (by which I do not
mean that such a justification can be found).[161]

Science prides itself on its objectivity, he is saying, but it is based
on faith – the faith in 'the absolute value of the true'. At the
time his was a voice crying in the wilderness, but twentieth-
century philosophers of science such as Thomas Kuhn and
Imre Lakatos have put flesh on his insight here that a science
without assumptions is absurd, even if they have not always
gone along with him in his argument that the desire to know
is to be counted as a form of intellectual lechery or gluttony.

But that is how Nietzsche operates. He is passionate
in his arguments because he feels that so much is at stake.
In 'On the Use and Abuse of History' his target is as much
the consumer of 'scientific' history as the researcher. To have
Ranke's attitude to history, he argues, is to feel that history *has
already happened*, that it is over and done with. Our curiosity
about the past knows no bounds, but because it has nothing
to do with us no aspect of it means more to us than any other:
ancient China, Byzantium, the life of Nell Gwyn or Frederick
the Great – all are equally fascinating. But soon we grow tired,
for we sense that however much we read there will always be
more. We are bombarded by a million possibilities but since
no one possibility means more to us than any other we fall
back, satiated but unsatisfied.

Today such arguments are commonplace in critiques of the
internet and its effect on a whole generation. In Nietzsche's
day they were unheard of. We know too much, he says, yet
what is such knowledge *for*? Think of forgetting, he says:

---

16 Friedrich Nietzsche, *The Genealogy of Morals*, tr. Francis Golfing
(New York, 1956), pp.186–7.

Forgetting is essential to action of any kind, just as not only light but darkness is essential for the life of everything organic. A man who wanted to feel historically through and through would be like one forcibly deprived of sleep... Thus it is possible to live almost without memory, and to live happily, moreover, as the animal demonstrates; but it is altogether impossible to live at all without forgetting. (62)

This cannot help reminding us of Borges' stricken youth or of Luria's poor mnemonist, unable ever to forget even when he wrote things down and then burned the page he had written. But the important point Nietzsche is making is that, when reading as when writing history the accumulation of facts will not help us understand. Believing it will makes us as vulnerable to populist calls as the person who reads no history at all. In the end we have to be awake to the demands of the present as of the past and to be prepared to change our minds, always recognising that we could well have been wrong in our prior assumptions. In each case the question is of the right balance between remembering and forgetting, between waking and sleeping, between that which can help us live, can invigorate our activity as Goethe put it, and that which paralyses us. But as our glance at some of these case studies has shown, there are always individual needs and desires at play, individual pressures and individual responses. That accommodation, that finding of the right balance, is going to be different in each and every instance, but accommodation there will have to be.

Interlude

AN ACT OF DESTRUCTION

I have thought about it so often that I no longer know if it is really my story, a part of my life.

I recall, or think I recall, myself standing in the kitchen of the ground-floor flat in Putney in which we lived after I left school and during my time at university, standing at the sink and slowly and methodically tearing the pages out of a scrapbook, and, as I do so, setting a match to each and watching it brown, burst into flame and turn to ash, fluttering down into the sink to be washed away by a jet of cold water. I recall, or think I recall, the mingled horror and triumph which took hold of me as I worked, and my refusal to think through the implications of what I was doing, as though I knew I had to act before I allowed myself to understand what it was I had done. But I recall nothing of the smell of the burnt paper or the mess it must have made of the sink, the charred fragments rising up and floating in the air before settling on the floor, on my clothes, no doubt, and on the sink itself. Did I have to spend hours cleaning up after my act of destruction or was it all quite easy, the work of a few minutes? I have no recollection.

You went up some shallow steps to reach the front door of the Victorian villa which had been split into three flats. Inside there was a small entrance hall and, on the right, a staircase leading to the two upstairs flats. Straight ahead was the door to the flat I shared with my mother. Inside, on the left, looking down St John's Road towards the church, was my mother's bedroom. Along the corridor and down a few steps was my room, giving onto a long, neglected garden at the end of which a high concrete wall abutted onto the rear of the platform of the East Putney underground station. Next to the bedroom was the bathroom and then down the stairs again was the ground floor/basement, with a windowless coal-room at the bottom of the stairs and, off to the left, a low-ceilinged but generous living-room and a kitchen. The windows of these two rooms were on a level with the garden, to which a door from the kitchen led, up a few steps.

It was in this kitchen that the act of vandalism took place. I recall, or think I recall, looking out at the sad lawn and the high grey wall at the end of it as I held the burning sheets over the grimy sink and the smell of burning filled the air.

Not that I wished to hide anything. When my mother came home, exhausted from her day's work, I made her a cup of tea and then told her what I had done. Her response was totally unexpected – neither tears nor anger, only the words: 'But it was mine as well as yours. How could you?'

I had never thought of it as hers. It was a large scrapbook with red cardboard covers in which the two of us had lovingly pasted newspaper accounts of my sporting exploits – in the swimming pool, on the athletics track, the football field, the tennis court – along with photos of me in action or, track-suited and smiling, receiving medals from the uniformed officers who always seemed to be presiding over such events. We had included it, along with a small but heavy box of medals, in the few suitcases we had taken with us on our departure from Egypt in the summer of 1956, though whether at my insistence or hers I could no longer remember. Whichever it was, it had come with us on our journey to a world we did not know and were unsure would welcome us or ever give us permanent shelter. It had been with us the year we had spent in Cheltenham, where I had studied for my A-levels and managed to obtain a State Scholarship and a place to read English at an Oxford college – and thus ensured – eventually

– our permanent residence in the country. It had come with us to the flat in Putney where we had settled so that in the year between school and university I could discover what a big city (I had never lived in one) could offer to those with very little money and an immense appetite for the culture we both felt we had been deprived of in the years I was growing up in Egypt.

And now I had destroyed it, wilfully and deliberately, and it had not been mine alone. It had been my mother's as well, to add to her meagre store of memorials, along with the big envelope of photographs she had carried with her throughout the eleven years she had spent in France, from 1934 to 1945 – photographs of her mother and father, long since dead, of her grandparents, her sister and her aunt, photographs of her and my father in their time in France together, both before my birth and after, photographs of me as a baby in her arms or in my tank-like pram, me on the beach in Nice and in the Massif Central resort of La Bourboule, where we had sought shelter during the last years of the war.

My mother never spoke of the burning of the scrapbook again. Perhaps the memory of it was too painful. Having lost so much in her life – her father at the age of five, her mother at the age of ten, her baby daughter from malnutrition in France during the war, not to speak of her husband's desertion – she knew much better than I did, though she was anything but nostalgic, the importance of mementos. But I went on thinking about it. Not all the time, but every now and again, with a stab of pain at the memory and a puzzlement as to the motives that had driven me to act as I had.

Why had I done it? What had seized me? It had something to do with starting a new life. With not letting the past drag me down. But now, as I think about it, I realise that it was more complicated than that. Had I been more confident of what I could achieve I would not have needed to make this gesture. For that is what it was. A burning of the bridges, but also a way of propelling myself forward into the future. By doing what I had done I was forcing myself to forge a wholly new life for myself, uncontaminated by the past. To become the writer I wanted for some obscure reason to be.

And now, as I pen this, I suddenly become aware of something else that the act of destruction entailed. I had known, I now think, I must have known, that the scrapbook was really hers as well as mine, and that was one of the reasons why I had destroyed it. Probably, at some unconscious level, I needed to destroy that which linked the two of us so inextricably together, her loving encouragement of my sporting prowess, her collaboration with me in the making of the scrapbook. I can see that this was entirely innocent on her part, that she would not have encouraged me had she not seen that I enjoyed my achievements in the pool and on the tennis court, that her one wish was not for me to be successful but to be happy. Yet the fact that it was her desire bound me to her in ways I both longed for and longed to be free of. It was not my scrapbook and it was not hers, it was ours, and as such it had to be destroyed, for I suppose I obscurely felt that if I was to forge my new life that life would have to be mine alone.

Now, of course, I regret it. I regret the weakness that led me to feel that the only way to be free was to do something which would hurt her so, and regret of course the necessary irrevocability of it and the fact that I no longer have the scrapbook to show my son and grandsons. All I have left is the memory of the act of destruction, but even that may, by now, have taken on a mythic dimension which conceals as much as it reveals, like so many other memories in our lives.

THE BURIAL OF THE DEAD (I)

The rightful burial of the dead has been a theme of literature for as long as literature has existed.

Take the *Iliad*, the first and greatest of all Western epics. It opens with a sort of overture, a short passage in which the central themes of the poem are all touched upon in one extraordinary sentence:

> The wrath do thou sing, O goddess, of Peleus' son Achilles, that baneful wrath which brought countless woes upon the Achaeans and sent forth to Hades many valiant souls of warriors and made themselves to be a spoil for dogs and all manner of birds. (I.1–5)

To be a spoil for dogs and birds – in other words to lack a proper burial – is not the fate that should await a valiant warrior, but, as a result of Achilles' refusal to fight with the Achaeans because of a personal vendetta with their leader, Agamemnon, it is what overtakes many of them. And this, as the overture indicates, is the central theme of the poem: proper burial or the lack of it. It will end, first, with the proper burial of Achilles' beloved friend Patroclus, whose death leads him finally to enter the fray with his fellow Achaeans, and then with the proper burial of his enemy, Hector, son of Priam, King of Troy, the killer of Patroclus. At these funerals the lamentations of the living, especially the women, play a crucial part in the proper conduct of the burial. The first to vent her grief at Hector's funeral is Andromache, his wife, followed by Hecabe, his mother, and finally by Helen, his sister-in-law and the cause of the whole war:

Hector, far dearest to my heart of all my husband's brethren! In sooth my husband is godlike Alexander, that brought me to Troy-land – would I had died ere then! For this is now the twentieth year from the time when I went from thence and am gone from my native land, but never yet heard I evil or despiteful word from thee... Therefore I wail for thee and for my helpless self with grief at heart; for no longer have I anyone beside me in broad Troy that is gentle to me or kind, but all men shudder at me. (XXIV 760–76)

These eruptions by women into a poem dominated by men are always desperately moving. After all the fighting and boasting we are, at such moments, brought face to face with human fear and loss and with the love and fondness of mothers for their children (Andromache in Book VI), of wives for their husbands, or, as here, of a wife for her husband's brother.

'So spake she wailing', the poet remarks as she concludes her lament, 'and thereat the countless throng made moan'. Clearly this is more than a private outpouring of grief but part of an orchestrated lamentation. In Book XIX, at the burial of Patroclus, for example, we have the same sequence as first Achilles' concubine Briseis throws herself on Patroclus' body and utters a great lament, and, when she has finished, 'thereto the women added their laments' (282-301). But Homer's verse moves on in its majestic hexameters, leaving us to imagine the details of the wailing for ourselves. The Athenian dramatists of the following centuries are not so restrained. The great scenes of lamentation and mourning for the dead in Aeschylus' *Libation Bearers* and Euripides' *Trojan Women* are full of onomatopoeic words, *otototoi, aiai aiai, ea ea,* and so on. At the climax to the earliest extant play, Aeschylus' *Persians*, Xerxes, the King, and the chorus of Persian elders lament the fate of their army, defeated and destroyed by the Greeks:

Xerxes:	Utter words of grief and sorrow,
	Full of lamentation; for this divinity
	Has turned right round against me.
	....
Chorus:	Cry 'oioioi' and learn it all.
	Where are the rest, your multitude of friends?
	Where are those who stood beside you,
	Men such as Pharandaces was,
	Susas, Pelagon and Damatas...?
	....
Xerxes:	Ió, Ió, ah me!
	After setting eyes on ancient Athens,
	Hateful Athens, all of them in one stroke,
	È è è è, gasp their life out wretchedly on the shore...
Chorus:	They have gone oi! – without a name.
Xerxes:	Ieh, ieh! Ió, Ió!
Chorus:	Ió, ió, you gods,
	You who have caused suffering that no-one expected
	For all to behold!...
Xerxes:	Cry out now in response to my cries.
Chorus:	A sad answer of sad sounds to sad sound [*dosin kakan kakōn kakois*].
Xerxes:	Raise a song of woe, joining it together with mine.
Xer & Cho:	Otototototoi! (941–1043)[17]

The English translation inevitably limps along, but at least it registers the places where the words give way to ritualised

---

17 Aeschylus, *Persians*, tr. Alan H.Sommerstein (Loeb Classical Library; London, 2008).

lamentations and conveys something of the impact the play must have made when first staged.

Robert Pogue Harrison, in his fine book on the importance of burial and burial rituals in human culture,[18] compares this to a lament of a girl for her brother from southern Italy collected and transcribed by the great Italian ethnographer, Ernesto de Martino and published by him in his remarkable book, *Morte e pianto rituale del mondo antico* (1958):

O my Francesco, O fair
O brother, O brother
O my Francesco, O brother, O brother
How will I cope, O fair
O my brother, O my brother, How I love him![19]

The lament, as de Martino shows at exhaustive length, helps the bereaved move from the animal to the human, from that which has been wrenched out of the social by grief to its reintegration in society. He is at pains to point out that simply reading a transcript of a funeral lament from the kind of peasant society he found in southern Italy and in Romania in the immediate post-war period can give one very little sense of what is going on. For these laments depend on three things: ritualised gestures, ritualised melodies and ritualised words and phrases. But – and that is one of the many fascinating

18   Robert Pogue Harrison, *The Dominion of the Dead* (Chicago; 2003).
19   Ernesto de Martino, *Morte e Pianto Rituale nel Mondo Antico* (Torino; 2014), pp.90–1. I am grateful to Robert Pogue Harrison's *The Dominion of the Dead* for putting me on to this wonderful book which has rarely been out of print in Italy since its first publication, but has yet to appear in English.

things to emerge from his detailed examination of these laments *in situ* – the very precision of the choreography of the rituals allows for moments of improvisation, enabling individual details – about the kindness of the deceased or the number of cattle he had – to emerge and be integrated into the ritual. Not only that. Describing the funeral of a priest in a Romanian village, he notes that one of the mourners would break off to admonish her friends: 'Keep going, Keep going. The gentlemen have to write in their books.' At another time one or two would interrupt their lamentation to finger admiringly the cloth of 'the gentlemen's' suits before slipping back into the lament.

To us all this may seem distasteful if not downright bizarre.[20] We tend to operate, here too, with a simple binary of either heartfelt and genuine or false and hypocritical, but a study like de Martino's should alert us to the fact that this is the result of a mindset which has only been prevalent in the West since the seventeenth and eighteenth centuries and which was put in place by the Protestant revolution of the

---

20 Dostoevsky provides a striking example of a nineteenth-century Jewish parallel to de Martino's twentieth-century Christian peasants in *From the House of the Dead*. 'I once asked Fomich what the sobbing meant and then the sudden transition to happiness and bliss' in his Sabbath devotions. 'He… explained that the weeping and sobbing stood for the thought of Jerusalem's loss, and that the Law prescribed the most violent sobbing and breast-beating at this thought. But at the moment of the very loudest sobbing, he, Isaiah Fomich, *must suddenly*, as it were by chance (this suddenness was also enjoined by the Law) *must suddenly* remember that there is a prophecy concerning the return of the Jews to Jerusalem. Then he must immediately burst out into rejoicing, song, laughter, and recite the prayers in such a way that his voice expressed the greatest possible happiness and his face the greatest triumph and nobility.'

sixteenth. De Martino's peasants, on the other hand, and their predecessors in the ancient world of the Mediterranean (he has a fascinating account of a present-day Egyptian Moslem funeral) would have made no sense of this opposition. The task of the funeral as a whole and of the funeral lament in particular, is to help the bereaved, broken by grief (as we see Achilles in the *Iliad* broken by his grief for Patroclus), incapable of speech, driven either to mutism or to howls of agony by the death of a loved one, to overcome this and return to life in the community. These rituals, which de Martino calls 'cultural memory', a memory, that is, consisting of bodily movement, melody and words, enact both the death of the loved one and the torment of the bereaved, and in so doing allow a space to be created where the healing process can start to take place.

To return to the lament of the sister for her brother. As Harrison points out (60ff.), while the semantic content of the lament is minimal it is nevertheless crucial. First there is the assertion that brother and sister must go their separate ways, he into death ('Now you must go, O brother') and she back to life. But then comes the acknowledgement that soon she too will follow him: 'I must die too, O brother'. The lament charts the return of the wounded animal to the social, but changed now, recognising that the loss is irrevocable and accepting that its own turn will one day come. King David, in the Book of Samuel, puts the whole thing with devastating simplicity: 'I will go to him, but he will not come to me', he says, after he has lain silent and grief-stricken for a long time, unable to come to terms with the death of the child Bathsheba has just borne him (2 Samuel 12.23). *I will go to him but he will not come to me.*

But the funeral is in one sense not a terminal point at all. The tomb, once established, becomes the focus for further displays of grief and emotion. Once the funeral has taken place with its appropriate rituals and the body has been buried, a quite different relationship to the dead is established. There are special days in which they are remembered by fresh rituals enacted at their tombs, by bringing flowers or a ritual meal on the anniversary of their death, and so on. Here too what we witness is the work of cultural memory. And the important thing is that it allows the living to find peace and release from the torments of remembering for the rest of the year. As Nietzsche would say, it allows the survivors to sleep in between the ceremonies, and allows the dead to become benign presences rather than vengeful ghosts. Only he who forgets remembers, and older cultures devised rituals of remembrance that allowed us to forget.

*

As de Martino brilliantly shows, it is no coincidence that the episode of the shield of Achilles, forged for him by Hephaestus, follows on from Achilles' despair at the death of his beloved friend. The shield's depiction of the changing seasons argues de Martino, and of those who go about their business in the fields, helps us, as it will help Achilles, to recognise that the death of a loved one, devastating as it is for the bereaved, has to be placed in the wider context of a universe which goes its own way oblivious of human suffering and loss, and that for every person who dies there is one who is born. That of course has been the lesson of the *Iliad* throughout. Human beings, says the poet, are like leaves on a tree, 'one generation of men springeth up and another passeth away'. (VI.146–50) This is not the bitter cynicism of Ecclesiastes but rather a wise recognition of the way things are. And, de Martino suggests, within every ancient funerary lament and within every peasant funeral lies not just the lesson that the dead will not return to life but also the lesson that if the seed does not die there will be no growth in the spring. In other words, these funerals tap into the ancient Mediterranean myth of the dying god, whether he be Tammuz or Osiris or Jesus Christ.

It is a commonplace of modern cultural history that both Judaism and Christianity differentiated themselves from the other cults of the ancient Near East by their insistence that they were historical faiths, based on the singular action of God in history – leading Israel out of bondage in Egypt, sending mankind His only son to redeem them. And both faiths have fought tooth and nail to maintain this distinction from the nature religions of the region, with their cyclical view of history and their multiple gods. Yet in the central rites of both Judaism and Christianity an occasion, long gone, which might, but for the ritual, have faded into obscurity, is both recalled and re-enacted. And this is important. Just as the south Italian peasant mourning ritual is an action at the end of which something has changed, so with both the Passover meal in Judaism and the Easter ceremony in Christianity. Both commemorate the founding events of their faiths, singular events where great tragedy is averted by the intervention of God, and in both the ending is joyful – the Israelites, having been slaves to Pharaoh in Egypt, triumphantly cross the Red Sea into freedom; Jesus, having died, is resurrected. The sorrow and the joy, the dark and the light, are one here – without the one there would not, could not, be the other. Had Pharaoh not been on the point of annihilating the Israelites their escape would not be so miraculous; had Jesus not died, He would not have risen. In both cases, without the reason for lamentation there would be no reason for celebration.

It is because these ceremonies combine strict choreography with a certain open-endedness that they are not subject to the kind of manipulation we saw at work in the demagogic injunction to remember – the Holocaust, Kosovo, Bloody Sunday, etc. It is precisely because both the Easter service and the Passover meal are playful re-enactments rather than simple injunctions to remember that they acquire their efficacity. The debates in the early years of Protestantism between those who said the Mass was a *re-enactment* of Jesus's Passion and those who said it was merely a *remembering* were so bitter because they were about a great deal more than an abstract principle; they were about the very soul of Christianity.

Judaism, which has been more relaxed about these things, as is to be expected of a religion based on practice rather than belief, makes of its central story something to be celebrated primarily not in a place of worship but in the home. At the Passover *seder* a certain order (*seder* means order in Hebrew) is to be respected, but the meal would last so long if every word were read and every gesture carried out, especially since discussion and elaboration are encouraged throughout, that each family finds its own way through it, abridging here, making room for the new there, much as in the ritual funeral laments recorded by de Martino. And of course, since it is after all a long meal in which all who can should participate, from the oldest to the youngest, there will always be those who doze, those who talk among themselves, those who want to play and those who want to eat and get to bed. That is fine. They can all be accommodated, and the central thrust of the ceremony – to tell the story of the escape from bondage in Egypt to freedom in the desert on the other side of the Red Sea, partly to teach the young, partly also to have it re-affirmed by all that were it not for what happened *then* they would not be here *now*, so that past and present will be forever intertwined – the central thrust will, year upon year, have been realised. We may not believe that everything happened just as it is described in the Bible and at the Passover *seder*, but that does not matter, for our beliefs change over time and may harden from doubt to scepticism or go the other way. The important thing is that the ceremony take place and we take part. And the same, it seems to me, is true of the Easter ceremony, whether it takes place in the fevered atmosphere of the great monastery of Grottaferrata, south of Rome, the last of the many Byzantine-Greek monasteries which once dotted Sicily, Southern Italy and even Rome, and where, on Good Friday, the women who have come to worship gash themselves and tear their hair and cry their songs of lamentation at the death of their lord, or the staidest English parish church. Forgetting and remembering are not the issue, they can, as it were, take care of themselves. What is important is the carrying out of a ceremony where the boundary between real sorrow and playacting is, as in the ritual laments discussed by Ernesto de Martino, always fluid.

VII

TOMBSTONES, INSCRIPTIONS

Ritualised ceremonies, whether Remembrance Day ceremonies annually remembering the dead of two world wars, or the private ceremonies of individuals visiting their own dead once a year, or the Jewish and Christian festivals of Passover and Easter – all these are, then, to be distinguished from the demagogic injunction not to forget. They are more robust, more able to tolerate doubt and confusion and complexity, more open to dialogue and so less open to abuse. Ritual of this kind, by making remembrance an act, something that takes place in the world, not in the mind or heart of the individual, frees us from the burden of continuous memory, allows us to forget as well as to remember.

But what of monuments to the dead? After all, just as it is human to bury the dead and mourn them, so it is human to feel the need to put up a stele or tombstone to mark the site of burial. What kind of memory is elicited by such objects?

Let the ending of *Beowulf*, the great Anglo-Saxon epic, stand for the principle:

Then the people of the Weders made a mound on the promontory, which was tall and broad, widely visible to mariners, and in ten days constructed a champion's monument, surrounded with a wall what the conflagration had left [Beowulf has been cremated, according to custom], as worthily as very prudent people could devise it. In the barrow they placed rings and brooches, all such ornaments as great-minded people had taken from the hoard: they left the earth holding warriors' treasure, gold in the dirt, where it now still resides, as useless to men as it was before. Then battle-brave sons of nobles rode round the mound, twelve in all, wanted to voice their grief and lament their kind, express it in words, and speak of the man. They praised his manliness and honoured his acts of heroism with glory – just as it is proper for a man to commend his friend and lord in speech, cherish him in his soul when he must be led forth from the flesh, just so the Geatish people, his retinue, bemoaned the fall of their lord, they said of worldly kings he was the most benevolent of men and the kindest, most generous to his people and most honour-bound. (ll.3156–82)[21]

There are three elements to the ritual. First of all a mound, tall and broad, 'widely visible to all mariners', must be raised up on the promontory where the king has been cremated. Then a wall is built round it, and within this are placed the treasures he will take with him into the afterlife as well of course as the bones that have survived the fire. Finally, twelve of his warriors ride round the monument, first praising the dead king's strength and heroic qualities and then recalling his human qualities of benevolence, kindness and generosity to his followers.

There is of course no extant tomb of Beowulf any more than there is one of Achilles. A great mound on the Trojan plain was associated with the cult of Achilles and it is said that Alexander, on his way to the East, worshipped there, but that is all. In later times, though, the practice became common of inscribing a name on a tombstone, along with the date of death and, if it was known, the date of birth as well and perhaps a brief account of the life of the buried person. On the tombstones of Roman soldiers of the first and second centuries C.E. we usually find some mention of the man's date

---

21 I use R.D. Fulk's elegant prose translation in *The Beowulf Manuscript* (Harvard; 2010).

of enlistment and rank. On early Christian tombstones we find some sort of Christian symbol, the fish or the cross, and, later, when Christianity became the state religion, a stylised inscription, taken from the liturgy. One such tombstone, found in Egypt, which commemorates a monk called Schenute, is surprisingly loquacious. It begins with the doxology, 'In the name of the Father and the Son and the Holy Ghost, Amen', which is repeated at the end. Then:

> May the God of the spirit and of all flesh, Who has overcome death and trodden Hades under foot and has graciously bestowed life on the world, permit the soul of Father Schenute to rest in the bosom of Abraham, Isaac and Jacob in the place of light and of refreshment where affliction pain and grief are no more. O gracious God the lover of men forgive him all the errors which he has committed by word act or thought. There is indeed no earthly pilgrim who has not sinned for Thou alone O God art free from every sin. In the name of the Father the Son and the Holy Ghost.

It concludes with a petition by the scribe: 'O Saviour give peace also to the scribe.'

So, in burial grounds all over Europe, the custom was established to inscribe something (not usually so elaborate) on the tombstone, and it lasts to this day. Yet by the middle of the eighteenth century we begin to find, among poets and novelists, a curious anxiety arising about the nature and role of gravestones and inscriptions. This connects in interesting ways with the transition we have been exploring from old to new ways of looking at the self and therefore of remembering and forgetting.

Thomas Gray's 'Elegy Written in a Country Churchyard' (1751) is so well-known and so full of lines that have become part of English culture that it is difficult to see clearly what it is saying. Obviously it is in the first place about a small English country churchyard where the poet is discovered meditating on the lives of the simple villagers who have found there their final resting-place, and as he does so asserting that they are as worthy of commemoration as the men whose deeds have earned them a place in the history books:

> Full many a flower is born to blush unseen
> > And waste its sweetness on the desert air.
> Some village-Hampden that with dauntless breast
> > The little Tyrant of his fields withstood;
> Some mute inglorious Milton here may rest,
> > Some Cromwell guiltless of his country's blood.

But the tone of the whole poem is much less easy to gage. It's true that it ends with the pious sentiment that all, whether famous or, like these, anonymous, rest 'in the bosom of his Father and his God', while the steady beat of the rhymed stanzas suggest a comfortable certainty. But this is belied by both the opening and the closing of the poem:

> The Curfew tolls the knell of parting day,
> > The lowing herd winds slowly o'er the lea,
> The plowman homeward plods his weary way,
> > And leaves the world to darkness and to me.
>
> Now fades the glimmering landscape on the sight,
> > And all the air a solemn stillness holds,
> Save where the beetle wings his droning flight
> > And drowsy tinklings lull the distant folds.

Here, where a solitary owl 'does to the moon complain':

> Beneath these rugged elms, that yew-tree's shade
> > Where heaves the turf in many a mould'ring heap,

> Each in his narrow cell for ever laid
> > The rude Forefathers of the hamlet sleep.

The lines evoke a shudder, and they are meant to. Though the argument of the poem is that the lives of these men and women were worth as much as those of the noble and the famous, the underlying feeling is that anything is better than this. Though ostensibly Christian, the poem is anything but in its sense of the utter desolation of death and the infinite sorrow at what it leaves behind:

> For them no more the blazing hearth shall burn,
> > Or busy housewife ply her evening care;
> No children run to lisp their sire's return,
> > Or climb his knees an envious kiss to share.

Faced with death the poet does not, like Homer, feel that as the leaves fall from the tree in the autumn so human lives pass away and new ones replace them (a recognition that is strangely consoling in that it integrates mankind into the larger rhythm of the universe), but he feels rather a pang of pain at the thought that he too will one day come to this. And that is the hub of it: ostensibly about the innate nobility of modern villagers, no matter how poor and overlooked by those who run the country, it is actually a poem about the poet's fear of oblivion. And it ends, indeed, with him imagining his death, imagining what will be said about him after his death, and even imagining the inscription on his tomb, which here turns into a veritable *apologia pro vita sua*:

> For Science frown'd not on his humble birth,
> And Melancholy marked him for her own.

Large was his bounty, and his soul sincere,
Heav'n did a recompence as largely send:
He gave to Mis'ry all he had, a tear,
He gain'd from Heav'n ('twas all he wish'd) a friend.

Something has clearly gone wrong with the culture surrounding tombs and burial. They function in this poem largely as triggers for melancholy brooding rather than as memorials. They no longer appear to form a meaningful part of the life of the community; though public, they speak of the secret, hidden life of the individual, alone in a frightening universe, with even God a far from certain friend. The object may be the same, but we are in a different universe from the one inhabited by the Egyptian monk Schenute and his scribe.

In 1936 the art historian Erwin Panofsky published an essay in Germany which was later, after he had settled in Princeton, to form a part of his most influential book, *Meaning in the Visual Arts*. The essay is entitled '*Et in Arcadia Ego*: Poussin and the Elegiac Tradition', and in it Panofsky traces the transformation of that phrase, which by the time of Poussin had become popular as an inscription on tombstones, from what every classicist would understand as 'Even in Arcady there was I', to the way it is commonly understood: 'I too was once in Arcady.' The first must be spoken by Death and is an unequivocal *memento mori*: even in so idyllic a place as Arcadia we will find Death. The second is usually taken as being spoken by the one inside the tomb and suggests that the dead person was once alive and a denizen of the blissful glades of Arcadia. In a wonderful bit of cultural detective work Panofsky traces the origin of the second meaning, the one that became prevalent in the eighteenth century, to the influence of two men, Virgil and Poussin.

It was, he says, Virgil in his *Eclogues* who invented Arcadia:

In Virgil's ideal Arcady human suffering and superhumanly perfect surroundings create a dissonance. This dissonance, once felt, had to be resolved, and it was resolved in that vespertinal mixture of sadness and tranquillity which is perhaps Virgil's most personal contribution to poetry. With only slight exaggeration one might say that he 'discovered' the evening.[22]

What Virgil does, Panofsky suggests, is not so much to exclude loss and death as to 'deprive them of their factuality': 'He projects tragedy either into the future, or preferably into the past, and he thereby transforms mythical truth into elegiac sentiment.' And it is this discovery of the elegiac, he argues which inaugurates the long line of poetry that was to culminate in Thomas Gray.

In the Middle Ages, though, this aspect of Virgil passed into oblivion (though Panofsky does not mention the extraordinary way Dante both recognises its power yet puts it firmly in its place in the figure of Virgil in the *Commedia*). It was Poussin, he argues, who seized on an as yet undefined feeling in the air and gave a new impetus to the elegiac tradition, and it is his great painting (there are two versions, but it is the later (1637) one in the Louvre that provides the fullest expression of the subject) of wayfarers absorbed 'in calm discussion and pensive contemplation' of a tomb on which the inscription *Et in Arcadia Ego* can be made out. And in Poussin's eighteenth century followers the trope became more and more simplified: not an inscription on a tombstone but a voice within the tomb is crying out: 'Alas, I too lived in Arcady where you now live; I too enjoyed the pleasures you now enjoy – and now I am dead and buried.' We are here on the threshold of Romanticism, says Panofsky, and he leaves us with a quotation from Johann

22   Erwin Panofsky, '*Et in Arcadia Ego*: Poussin and the Elegiac Tradition', in *Meaning in the Visual Arts* (London; 1970), p.346.

Georg Jacobi's *Winterreise* of 1769: 'Whenever, in a beautiful landscape, I encounter a tomb with the inscription *Auch war ich in Arkadien* I point it out to my friends; we stop a moment, press each other's hands, and proceed.'[23]

*

The first two volumes of *Tristram Shandy* were published in 1760, less than a decade after Gray published his 'Elegy', and in the early pages of the very first volume we find Sterne exploring, in his own inimitable way, the nexus of sentiments surrounding cemeteries and gravestones that were Gray's theme in his poem.

In the course of discussing hobby-horses and midwives Tristram comes to talk of the local parson and his horse, the latter, he informs us, a veritable brother of Don Quixote's nag Rosinante[24]. This leads him to tell us (or perhaps suddenly to decide, for the book captures wonderfully well the free play of the mind exploring its fictional subject and there is no reason to doubt that it reflects the extempore nature of the writing of the book itself) that the parson's name was Yorick. And Sterne goes on to invent a splendid genealogy for him, playing all the while on the reader's knowledge of *Hamlet* and *Hamlet* scholarship. Yorick's family, he says, seems to have been of Danish extraction and came to England 'as early as the reign of Horwendilas, king of Denmark, in whose court... an ancestor of Mr *Yorick's*... held a considerable post to the day of his death.' The record does not say what this post was, continues Sterne, but 'it has often come into my head that this post could be none other than that of the King's chief Jester;

---

23   *Ibid.*, p.366.
24   The following paragraphs are reworked from my book, *Hamlet Fold on Fold* (London; 2016).

and that *Hamlet*'s *Yorick*, in our Shakespeare, many of whose plays, you know, are founded upon *authenticated* facts – was certainly the very man.'

Now Yorick of course appears in *Hamlet* only as a skull held up for inspection by the Gravedigger. However, he is conjured up for us in some of the most famous lines in the play. The Gravedigger produces the skull as evidence of how long a man may lie in the ground before he rots, and when Hamlet asks whose skull it is, replies: 'A pestilence on him for a mad rogue! 'A [he] poured a flagon of Rhenish wine on my head once. This same skull was Yorick's skull, the Kings Jester.' 'Let me see,' says Hamlet, stretching out his hand for it. Then, taking it:

> Alas, poor Yorick, I knew him, Horatio, for a fellow of infinite jest, of most excellent fancy. He hath bore me on his back a thousand times, and now – how abhorred in my imagination it is. My gorge rises at it. Here hung those lips that I have kissed I know not how oft. Where be your gibes now, your gambols, your songs, your flashes of merriment that were wont to set the table on a roar? Not one now to mock your own grinning? Quite chop-fallen? Now get you to my lady's chamber, and tell her, let her paint an inch thick, to this favour she must come. (V.i)

Yorick, one of the most famous characters in Shakespeare, never appears in *Hamlet*; Shakespeare brings him to life with nothing but a skull and a few words. But what words! Because Hamlet has such a way with words and because what he says still chimes with us today we tend to remember his words and not those of the Gravedigger. But an interesting faultline has opened up between them, and by focussing only on Hamlet's words we fail perhaps to see it. The Gravedigger, in keeping with his profession, is totally without sentiment concerning the dead he has to deal with. He would not have given the skull another thought had Hamlet not asked him about it, and then his only memory of the living Yorick is that he poured a flagon of Rhenish wine on his head once. 'A pestilence on him for a mad rogue!' is his epitaph on the court jester. Hamlet, on the other hand, is already moving into the orbit of Gray's elegy: 'Alas, poor Yorick. I knew him well, Horatio, a fellow of infinite jest, of most excellent fancy. He hath bore me on his back a thousand times, and now - 'There is, it is true, still the late medieval horror of death in the *memento mori* theme he now develops: so was he once, and now this is what he has come to – remember, all of you – that is the theme of the latter half of his speech. But what we remember most are the opening words: 'Alas, poor Yorick', with its underlying implication: Alas, poor me, destined to the same end. Hamlet resonates with us precisely because he touches our modern sensibilities, though the play is careful to place his own view of himself within a rich context in order to make us, by the end, see both his remarkable qualities and his profound limitations.

Sterne seizes on the modern aspects and jokingly appropriates them for his own ends, pretending that the historical accuracy of Shakespeare's play will give credence to his own creation, knowing full well that the reader who knows *Hamlet* (and Sterne seems to assume that this means everyone who will read his own book) will know that the play is a fiction and the character of Yorick not just an invention of the author's but the product of the memory and rhetoric of another fictional character. Yet just as Shakespeare makes out of this a character in whom we immediately believe, so Sterne makes of his Yorick, this doubly unreal character, a wonderfully real, benign and eccentric presence, hovering over the dysfunctional Shandy family, a model, clearly, of what Sterne takes to be the good life:

The fact was this:– that instead of that cold phlegm and exact regularity of sense and humour, you could have look'd for, in one so extracted [i.e. of Danish extraction and descent], - he was, on the contrary, as mercurial and sublimated a composition, - as heteroclite a creature in all his declensions, - with as much life and whim, and *gaité de coeur* about him, as the kindliest climate could have engendered and put together... For, to speak the truth, Yorick had an invincible dislike and opposition in his nature to gravity; - not to gravity as such: for when gravity was wanted he would be the most grave or serious of mortal men for days and weeks together; but he was an enemy to the affectation of it, and declared war against it, only as it appeared a cloak for ignorance or folly; and then, whenever it fell in his way... he seldom gave it much quarter.

That this was Sterne's ideal and an attitude to the world with which he identified is attested by the remarkable fact that when he came to publish his own sermons he entitled them *The Sermons of Mr Yorick*. But it is a mark of his genius that he can only do so because, in the novel, he has taken steps to throw into question our whole attitude to sermons, since the book abounds in parody sermons, and, more importantly, our attitude to Yorick, both as he has been described here and as he comes to us through Hamlet's famous speech.

One way he does this is by incorporating the most famous sentence in that speech into his own book and, by so doing, raising questions not just about that book but also about *Hamlet*, about epitaphs and about mourning. For of course Sterne's Yorick, like his ancestor, has to die, and Sterne goes to town on a deathbed scene which, like so much of *Tristram Shandy*, is so written as to be both sentimental and a parody of sentimentality, making it impossible to decide which it finally is.

Eugenius, Yorick's friend, has come to visit him on his deathbed, and they exchange a few words:

Yorick's last breath was hanging upon his trembling lips, ready to depart as he uttered this, – yet still it was uttered with something of a *cervantick* tone; – and as he spoke it, *Eugenius* could perceive a stream of lambent fire lighted up for a moment in his eyes; – faint picture of those flashes of his spirit, which (as Shakespeare said of his ancestor) were wont to set the table in a roar.

Eugenius was convinced from this, that the heart of his friend was broke; he squeez'd his hand, – and then walk'd softly out of the room, weeping as he walk'd. *Yorick* followed *Eugenius* with his eyes to the door, – he then closed them, and never opened them more.

As so often in Sterne, we do not know whether to weep, to clap our hands at a bravura performance of 'the deathbed scene', or to laugh at how he has brought us and a character blatantly fashioned out of a few phrases in an old play to this pass.

But he is not done yet. The chapter continues:

He lies buried in a corner of his churchyard, in the parish of -, under a plain white marble slab, which his friend *Eugenius*, by leave of his executors, laid upon his grave, with no more than these three words of inscription serving both for his epitaph and elegy.

Alas, poor YORICK!

Ten times a day has *Yorick's* ghost the consolation to hear his monumental inscription read over with such a variety of plaintive tones, as denote a general pity and esteem for him; – a foot-way crossing the churchyard close by the side of his grave, – not a passenger goes by without stopping to cast a look upon it, and sighing as he walks on,

Alas, poor YORICK!

This is followed by the famous all-black page, presumably signifying the oblivion of death, before a new chapter begins.

A funerary monument is meant to outlast its occasion. That is why it is set up, usually in stone, and why the words that appear upon it are chiselled into the stone. It stands in sharp contrast to the immediate outpouring of grief that greets the death of a loved person or the choreography of grief that accompanies the coffin to the grave. Yet Sterne here tries, or pretends to try, to conflate the two. He presents us with an inscription enclosed in a black border, such as one still finds on the billboards of Catholic countries to announce a death, yet the tone of the inscription is startlingly at odds with this, for the 'alas' at the beginning and the exclamation mark at the end are an attempt (or the pretence of an attempt) to mimic the actual speech and intonation of the bereaved. At the same time the phrase flaunts itself as not just a precise mimicry of actual grief but also a quotation from an old and much-loved play. The result is something that does not succeed (and of course is not meant – or not *quite* meant – to succeed) in evoking either the grief of the bereaved or the dignity of the traditional epitaph. What it does do is to raise questions about where we stand – in Sterne's time and in our own – in relation to epitaphs, to death, and even to remembrance.

*

Cemeteries haunt the imagination of the eighteenth century, culminating in the terrifying graveyard encounter between Don Giovanni and the statue of the Commendatore, the man he has killed, in Mozart's great opera. Wordsworth, born in 1770 and thus one of a handful of fascinating figures who straddle the eighteenth and nineteenth centuries, is a particularly interesting case. For all the dozens of poems he devoted to places, where he is always at pains to tell his reader precisely where and when the piece was written – 'Lines Composed a Few Miles Above Tintern Abbey...July 23, 1798'; 'Sonnet Composed in one of the Valleys of Westmoreland on Easter Day'; 'Sonnet Composed on Westminster Bridge, September 3, 1802' – there are comparatively few composed in country churchyards, and most of these are mediocre, suggesting that unlike nature, human burials did not particularly stir him.

Yet Wordsworth was deeply concerned with these things, as is shown by the lengthy essay he devoted to the subject, 'Essay Upon Epitaphs'. 'Almost all the Nations have wished that certain external signs should point out the place where the dead are interred,' he begins. 'The custom, proceeded obviously from a twofold desire: first to guard the remnants of the deceased from irreverent approach or from savage violation; and secondly to preserve their memory.' Then, as soon as men had learned the use of letters, he suggests, they inscribed epitaphs upon these monuments. These, he goes on, must respect social conventions yet be personal; not too personal though, or too detailed, or the ignorant passer-by will not be able to identify with the dead. An extended and detailed portrait should be left to written elegies or memorial essays. As for epitaphs:

> Much better it is to fall short in discrimination, than to pursue it too far, or to labour it unfeelingly. For in no place are we so much disposed to dwell upon these points, of nature or condition,

wherein all men resemble each other as in the temple where the universal Father is worshipped or by the side of the grave which gathers all human Beings to itself, and 'equalises the lofty and the low'. We suffer and weep with the same heart, we love and are anxious for one another in one spirit, our hopes look to the same quarter; and the virtues by which we are all to be furthered and supported as patience, meekness, good-will, justice temperance and temperate desire, are in equal degree the concern of us all. Let an Epitaph, then, contain at least these acknowledgements of our common nature; or let the sense of their importance be sacrificed to a balance of opposite qualities or minute distinctions in individual character; which, if they do not (as will for the most part be the case), when examined, resolve themselves into a trick of words, will, even if they are true and just, for the most part, be grievously out of place; for as it is probable that few only have explored these intricacies of human nature so can the tracing of them be interesting only to a few.

What is striking here is not the sentiments expressed, which are of a piece with the views we find in the Preface to the *Lyrical Ballads*, but the fact that Wordsworth feels the need to articulate them. As with books of etiquette, one senses that when the need is felt to codify something, to explain what should or should not be done in so meticulous a fashion, a long-standing tradition is coming to an end. What we feel, reading this essay of Wordsworth's, as we feel reading *Tristram Shandy*, is that how epitaphs should be written and how they should be read, how we should respond to graves and gravestones – all this has suddenly become problematic.

And it is not difficult to see why. Wordsworth, like Gray, takes it for granted that what gravestones and epitaphs do is lead the passer-by to identify with the dead. But this was not the aim of the gravestone of the Egyptian monk Schenute. The emphasis there was on the salvation of his soul, and, as an afterthought, that of the scribe. We are not asked to identify with the dead but rather to add our prayers to the ones inscribed on the tomb. Not empathy but an action is asked of us. The gulf between the two sets of assumptions is unbridgeable.

VIII

'WHO IS THE MAN SITTING ON GENERAL GORDON?'

When my mother was a little girl growing up in the small Egyptian town of Helwan, just south of Cairo, she and her sister, who both adored animals, would often, she told me, be taken on a walk by their English nanny past an imposing equestrian statue. 'That is General Gordon', their nanny informed them, and there it rested until one day my inquisitive aunt asked: 'Nanny, who is the man sitting on General Gordon?'

Just as poets and novelists, always the best barometers of what is beginning to seem false in any society, were beginning to question the role and function of epitaphs on private tombstones, newly self-conscious nation-states were starting to put up monuments, often equestrian statues, to the men (nearly always men) they wished to honour. More statues were put up in the course of the nineteenth and early twentieth century than at any time since the High Middle Ages, when the exteriors of medieval cathedrals had been adorned with saints, figures from the Old and New Testaments and even signs of the zodiac. Mostly these were of soldiers who, the state felt, had died heroically fighting for their country, like Nelson on his column in Trafalgar Square or Gordon of Khartoum in Helwan, Egypt. Sometimes they were simply of men the state felt it needed to honour.

Most of the time, as Robert Musil noted in an essay on monuments he wrote in 1927, they were invisible. 'The remarkable thing about monuments,' he writes, 'is that one does not notice them. There is nothing so invisible as a monument.'

The very ubiquity of these monuments, in city squares and on street corners, and the growth of a population with little awareness of history and no strong investment in the fortune of the country, especially in wars in far-away places, 'effectively precipitate[s] them into an ocean of oblivion.'[25]

Monuments only become visible again when, for one reason or another, changes in perception in the society at large render them visible. This happened not long ago with the statue of Cecil Rhodes in Oxford. A request was put in to Oxford City Council to take down the statue as it commemorated a man who had brought suffering to thousands. The Council's response, and this was endorsed by most of the papers which took up the story, was that once you started, where did you stop? Should the statues of medieval kings and warriors, who had no doubt caused suffering to many, also be taken down? And was the response that no-one now alive was offended by them, whereas a great many people were offended by the statue of Cecil Rhodes, persuasive? Once, obviously, the statues of saints on medieval churches had caused offence, and this had resulted in the iconoclasm of the Reformation, when many of them were torn down, broken or defaced. But that, we now feel, was a form of vandalism which caused untold damage to Britain's rich heritage of medieval art. Do we risk the same thing happening with the art of the nineteenth and twentieth centuries? Even the most fervent antagonist of the latter-day iconoclasts did not put forward the defence that the statue of Rhodes was worth preserving as a work of art. But if it causes offence to some and is worthless as art, why not do away with it?

These are difficult if not impossible issues to resolve to everyone's satisfaction. We would rightly have no truck with

---

25   Robert Musil, 'Denkmale', in *Nachlass zu Leibzeiten*, quoted in Peter Carrier, *Holocaust Monuments and National Memory Cultures in France and Germany Since 1989* (Oxford; 2005) p.15.

the sensitive supporter of the Front National in France who asked for the removal of the plaques put up by the then President François Chirac on the frontage of institutions from which Jewish children had been deported by the Nazis with the active participation of the Vichy government on the grounds that there were many French patriots who refused to do such things and that the plaques were an offence to them. But what if Martine Le Pen were to become President? Would the argument then be that since the majority had voted for her and her policies, if one such policy was the removal of the plaques, it was right that in a democracy the will of the majority should be respected? The answer has to be that in mature democracies, though it is the majority that forms the government this does not give that government the right to ride roughshod over the established conventions of the country. The iconoclasm of the Reformation is, we hope, a thing of the past.

It can, however, flare up again at any moment. We all remember the images shown on television of the statues of Stalin and then later of Saddam Hussein being pulled down by jubilant crowds as a sign of the end of a hated era. In the democratic West, though, there is the feeling that even if statues still stand today of men history judges to be unworthy of the honour – if anyone still thinks of it as an honour – of having had a statue of themselves erected in a public place, it would in fact make too much of an issue out of it were isolated calls heeded for them to be pulled down. But how many voices would it take for the call to become something more compelling? And if that happened these monuments, instead of being invisible and so forgotten, would suddenly become all too visible as the focus of debate and confrontation.

Reviewing some books about the British in India and commenting on what he calls 'a tradition of cynical candour' among the British colonial administrators, Ferdinand Mount wrote: 'But the villainous Charles Napier, still secure today on his perch in Trafalgar Square, matched [Clive] for cynical candour: "We have no right to seize Sind. Yet we will do so, and a very advantageous, useful, human piece of rascality it will be."'[26] Yet Mount does not go on to call for the statue to be pulled down, though it stands in one of the most prominent public places in the British Isles. And why should he? I have passed through Trafalgar Square countless times, I have gazed up at the statue of Nelson on his column, but I have no idea who the other figures are who occupy the lower plinths in the square. And that surely holds for the vast bulk of those who throng the place every day of the year. And even if we knew that this particular statue was of someone called Napier even fewer would know anything about him.

Yet as recent events in America have shown, history does not simply flow on in an unbroken line. It can be stopped in its tracks at any moment and what had grown invisible because of habit and indifference can suddenly become not only visible but dangerously divisive.

*

One of the greatest novels of the twentieth century, William Faulkner's *The Sound and the Fury* (1929), is also one of the greatest novels about the American South. It deals with the disintegration of the white South's dream in the shape of one dysfunctional family, the Compsons: Jason Compson, the father who takes to drink as he sees the shattering of his dreams for a happily married life, for his sons to succeed him and do well, for his daughter to marry into a good family; his self-pitying, intensely selfish wife; and their four children, one, with speech and learning difficulties, habitually referred to as

---

26   Ferdinand Mount, *London Review of Books*, 7/9, 2017, p.7.

'the idiot'; the second who marries an odious man to hide an unwanted pregnancy; the third who commits suicide, unable to bear what is happening to his beloved sister; and the fourth, mean, self-pitying, hating the world around him for, as he sees it, ruining his life, who inherits what is left of the family fortune. Through it all the black family that serves them carry on their impoverished lives with at their centre the matriarch, Dilsey, whose humanity and compassion somehow survive intact despite what the family she serves put her through, buoyed up by the local church and its charismatic preachers who keep reminding the community that Jesus was, like them, an outcast and a sufferer.

In the last pages, on Easter Sunday, Luster, the black boy, drives Benjy, the 'idiot', now a man of thirty-three, to the cemetery to visit the grave of his dead brother:

> They approached the square, where the Confederate soldier gazed with empty eyes beneath his marble hand into wind and weather. Luster took still another notch in himself and gave the impervious Queenie a cut with the switch, casting his glance about the square. 'Dar Mr Jason's car,' he said, then he spied another group of negroes. 'Les show dem niggers how quality does, Benjy,' he said. 'Whut you say?' He looked back. Benjy sat, holding the flower in his fist, his gaze empty and untroubled. Luster hit Queenie again and swung her to the left at the monument.[27]

It is entirely appropriate that the book should end under the gaze of the stone soldier, his gaze as empty as the idiot's. Monuments like this one were ubiquitous throughout both North and South after the Civil War, and they served as the focal points of widespread remembrance ceremonies. But, as David Rieff reminds us:

---

27   William Faulkner, *The Sound and the Fury* (London; 1931), p.320.

As with every project focussed on historical remembrance whether the goal in any given instance is to forge it, sustain or affirm it, challenge it, reconstruct it, or replace it, there was nothing innocent about these commemorations. (11)

In fact, he goes on to say, it would be appropriate to use an expression much in vogue among French historians and call the erection of such monuments 'skirmishes in an ongoing memory war'. Strangely, given that the North won so decisively, it was the South that won the memory war in America. We have only to think of the enormous popularity of the film of *Gone with the Wind* to realise, as Caroline Janney, the foremost historian of this phenomenon, puts it, that 'Americans could not get enough of the romantic epic depicting white southern resolve in the face of defeat'.[28]

But while we all like a plucky loser, especially if he is dashing and romantic and has a moustache like Clark Gable's, that film and the entire narrative which grew up around the defeat of the South hid a much darker truth, one which has periodically surfaced in the course of American history and which, for the rest of the world, has emerged into the full light of day with the arrival in the White House of Donald Trump.

In June 2015 a young man called Dylan Roof walked into the evening service at the Emanuel African Methodist Episcopal Church in Charleston, Missouri, and opened fire, killing nine people including the senior pastor, Senator Clementa Pinckney. When he was arrested it became clear that Roof was a white supremacist still contesting the outcome of the Civil War a hundred and fifty years on. In the wake of the massacre it was decided to end the use of the Confederate flag where it was still flown and, in South Carolina, to stop it flying from the State Capitol. But that did not stop the statues

---

28   Quoted in Rieff, p.112.

of the Confederate dead and especially their leaders in the Civil War from becoming the focus of racial tension. In the summer of 2017 a large group of white supremacists and neo-Nazis descended, fully armed, on the town of Charlottesville in Virginia for a torchlit rally round the statue of the Confederate General, Robert E. Lee. In the ensuing clashes with protesters a young white woman protester was run down by a car driven by a supremacist and killed. President Trump, true as ever to his instincts, only reluctantly condemned the murder, alleging that there were 'good and bad people' on both sides. It was the first time an American president had not openly dissociated himself from white supremacists and racists in the country.

Ironically, the tragic incident seems to be leading to the taking down of Confederate statues in most of the Southern states as their potential for racist tension has grown clear. In the aftermath of the incident, too, journalists have been catching up with historians and trying to explain to the world that most of these statues actually went up not in the immediate aftermath of the Civil War but much later, usually in times of heightened racial tension. As Conrad West, a civil rights leader who spoke to the Guardian's Jason Wilson after the Charlottesville incident put it: 'We should have eliminated these statues a long time ago... The Confederacy is part of a tradition that's grounded in hatred, and is tied to one of the most vicious structures of domination in the modern world.'

What is so interesting as well as so frightening about what is happening in Trump's America is how it reveals that everything depends on perception. Without America's failure ever really to deal with its racial divide, without the rise of the extreme and intolerant right in the presidency of Donald Trump, these statues would have remained as neutral and harmless, as invisible, to use Musil's striking adjective, as the statue of General Gordon and his horse in the small Egyptian town of Helwan or of Charles Napier in Trafalgar

Square. But, of course, these could become the focus of anger and resentment at any moment, if circumstances changed and unscrupulous politicians and men full of resentment and self-pity chose to make them so. For we are not here talking about actual memory or about the past but about the anger and bigotry that always lurks beneath the surface of even the most placid-seeming modern societies, and that will latch on to anything to support its view of the world.

IX

MEMORIAL MONUMENTS

The statue of Nelson in Trafalgar Square is a tribute to a military leader but it is also, and primarily, a national monument. Tellingly, it was erected not at Nelson's death in 1805 but in the 1840s, and it stands, tall on its column in the heart of London, as a symbol of the might of the British Empire. The nineteenth century is full of such symbols of a nation's power, from the Arc de Triomphe in the heart of Paris, begun in 1806 to celebrate Napoleon's victory at the Battle of Austerlitz but only competed in 1836, to the Victory Column in Berlin commissioned in 1866 to celebrate the Prussian triumph in the Prusso-Danish War and completed (with the addition of the golden statue of the Goddess of Victory on the top) in 1873, after further Prussian triumphs over the Austrians and the French. Along with multiple statues of fallen soldiers the newly self-aware nation states could not, it seems, stop erecting monuments to themselves. And this of course continued especially in the totalitarian countries of Eastern Europe and the Middle East, right through the twentieth century.

Yet the monument that became the sign of a new era, in the wake of the decimation of human life in the First Word War which made all forms of triumphalism suspect, was the Tomb of the Unknown Soldier, erected first in France and Britain and then in most of the world's major countries (in France it lies directly under the Arc de Triomphe), testifying to the loss of young men in that war in such horrifying numbers that most of them have no individual graves and only a corporate and anonymous identity. Such monuments, though, were still conceived and executed in the old ways, as though those who commissioned and erected them had not yet caught up, imaginatively, with what had just happened. After the Second World War, however a radical change occurred though whether that was the result of the peculiar horror of the Nazi atrocities or because it simply takes time for the civic imagination to catch up with what artists had intuited long before it is impossible to determine. James Young's remarkable book *The Texture of Memory*, a study of Holocaust memorials erected in Germany, Austria, Poland, Israel and the United States in the years between the end of the war and the fall of the Berlin Wall in 1989, examines some of the reasons for the change and explores the innovative solutions devised by artists and architects commissioned, especially in Germany, by enlightened civic bodies.[29]

Among the many evocative photos in Young's book one in particular resonates. It shows a man dressed in an anonymous buttoned-up overcoat, scarf and cap, holding a briefcase in his right hand, walking through a derelict cemetery, a few tombstones still standing but the majority flattened, though whether by bombing or desecration it is impossible to say and, beyond, a few poor trees and houses set in flat fields which stretch to the horizon. The caption tells us that this is a survivor returning to his hometown of Chmelnik after the war. I don't think I have ever seen a photograph that so poignantly conveys the sense of loss caused by war and raises so urgently the question of how on earth to compensate such a person.

The simple answer of course is that nothing can. But in the countries that had been devastated by the war, particularly

---

29   James E. Young, *The Texture of Memory: Holocaust Memorials and Meaning* (London; 1994).

Germany and Poland, governments and civic bodies hurried to erect monuments to the victims. In West Germany this led to massive soul-searching. Until then, after all, monuments had been erected to the heroes and victims of the nations that erected them, but now West Germany was seeking to build monuments to those, not always its own citizens, who had been victimised by the German state itself. How was this to be done?

A further, though for a long time unnoticed complication was that the culture of deference which had prevailed throughout the nineteenth and early twentieth centuries had been eroded by the two world wars. No longer could a country's rulers impose civic monuments on a largely passive populace. Now everyone wanted to have their say, including of course, those commissioned to build the new monuments. For them, the architects and sculptors, Lewis Mumford's dictum that 'If it's a monument it's not modern; if it's modern it cannot be a monument', was, if not self-evident then at least at the forefront of their thinking. Monuments, which had already started to be derided by the avant-garde before the First World War, had, of course, been thoroughly debased by Fascist regimes in the preceding half-century. Yet the need to commemorate was urgently felt, and not just by the victims. What was to be done? Young discusses dozens of solutions, from self-destroying monuments to spaces left deliberately empty, but none seem really satisfactory. Survivors dislike abstraction, he points out, yet the makers of monuments need it if they are to escape the dead weight of traditional solutions. How to satisfy both parties?

Young is pessimistic. Or rather, he favours what he calls 'memory-work', the ensemble of questions that arise around the *creation* of these monuments, the competitions, the outcries, the letters to the press and all the rest of what has accompanied each of these works, rather than the monument itself. Somehow, he feels, this public debate is truer to what everyone is after than any finished work could ever be. He also shows how, in both Poland and Israel, as opposed to West Germany, the state did what states always do, it pre-empted the monuments for its own purposes; in Poland systematically downplaying the extent of Jewish massacres and insisting on parity between Polish and Jewish suffering, and in Israel constructing a narrative in which the decimation of the Jews in Europe during the war and the creation of the state of Israel were two sides of the same coin. This is the old story of what Rieff calls the politicisation of memory. East Germany, like the Soviet bloc as a whole, had its own narrative of heroic resistance to Fascism and thus stuck to the old forms. West Germany's attitude to its post-war monuments, on the other hand, has been markedly different and has much to teach us.

Early on in his book Young remarks that 'The more memory comes to rest in exteriorized forms the less is it experienced internally.' Where have we come across this sentiment before? Why, in Sterne's ironical exploration of the epitaph on Yorick's tombstone. And as we saw there, the desire for more immediacy, for internal feeling (the heart) rather than external fact (the stone) springs from a loss of faith in the ability of tradition to do its work. Young continues: 'In shouldering the memory-work monuments may relieve viewers of their memory burden.' This he sees as a failing, but if, as I have been arguing, we see it as the primary aim of monuments, just as it is the aim of ritual burial, to 'shoulder the memory-work', then our whole attitude to contemporary monuments will change. We will then ask: Is it possible for a public monument to do this work for us today just as ancient ways of burial and commemoration once did for our ancestors, or does the loss of unified communities, communities, that is, sharing common aims and assumptions, mean that all monuments will inevitably be either felt as irrelevant or, at best, as messy compromises between competing visions?

That is certainly the view of Peter Carrier, whose book, *Holocaust and National Memory in France and Germany since 1989* published in 2005, in a sense brings Young, whose book came out in 1993, up to date. Carrier concentrates on just two monuments, the Vel' d'Hiv monument in Paris, so called because it is built on the site of the infamous holding station for Jews waiting to be deported to the camps in Poland in the winter velodrome, and the Holocaust Memorial in Berlin. Speaking of the latter and of President Kohl's cancellation of the first competition for a suitable monument set up in 1995 on the grounds that there was insufficient consensus behind the shortlisted entries, and his call for a new one to be instituted, Carrier writes:

> The competition of 1997 was therefore handicapped from the start by an ideological burden, based on the demand that a single monument should embody the whole nation's memory of the genocide against the Jews during the Second Word War, and on the consistent demand for consensus... The petitions highlighted the indeterminate and therefore problematic social appeal of this political symbol. Can a nation be conceived as a coherent community that identifies collectively with or engages in a sense of emotional allegiance with a single central symbol? And are the monuments politically legitimate forms of cultural expression that reflect the values of consciousness of a national community?[30]

His answer to both questions is a resounding no. But I feel that he reaches this conclusion only because he starts from the wrong premise. Like Young, and like Tristram Shandy, he asks too much of monuments because he no longer understands the role monuments played in traditional cultures. To my

---

30   Peter Carrier, *Holocaust Monuments and National Memory Cultures in France and Germany since 1989* (New York; 2005).

mind, if one comes to the Berlin Holocaust Memorial with an open mind one may discover that it triumphantly vindicates Chancellor Kohl, and it does this not by some sleight of hand such as creating a 'negative space' or a purely conceptual object but because its creators have understood profoundly what that role once was and thus found how to make not a replica but an equivalent for our modern, fragmented world.

Everything seemed to militate against success, as Carrier demonstrates at exhaustive length, yet, as always happens, art, if it is good enough, finds answers where theoreticians and historians can only see an impasse. If we will only trust the artwork we may discover that the answer to Carrier's second question (only removing the words 'nation' and 'national' from its formulation) can in fact be yes.

*

The Memorial to the Murdered Jews of Europe, to give it its full title, lies in the heart of Berlin just south of the Brandenburg Gate and between the Tiergarten to the West and the grid of streets of the old East Berlin to the East. Designed by the architect Peter Eisenman, the sculptor Richard Serra (at first), and the engineer Bruno Hoppold, it covers a trapezium field of 69,000 square metres (roughly the site of three football fields), and consists of 2,700 grey concrete stelae 2.38 metres long, 95 centimetres wide and between 50 and 500 centimetres in height. The blocks are laid in a grid pattern, 54 rows going from north to south and 67 from east to west, arranged in straight lines 95 centimetres apart. The ground of the field undulates continuously though there is a marked dip towards the middle, but, because of the increasing height of the stelae as one penetrates the rows, when seen from the outside the field appears merely to rise and fall in gentle waves just a little above ground level. An attached Information Centre contains the names of some three million Jewish victims and other information. Begun in 2003, the Memorial was inaugurated in May 2005, sixty years after the end of the Second World War.

The genius of the installation lies in the unpredictable undulation of the ground and in the varying height of the blocks. This means that around the periphery they can serve as benches on which one can sit and children run around and play. But imperceptibly, as one ventures down the alleys, the blocks rise higher and higher until one is walking through them as through a forest of concrete. At the same time, though they are laid in regular rows, the blocks never sit in the ground at quite the same angle, so that the light catches the tops in different ways, leading to a further sense of disorientation. The cries and laughter of children playing on the periphery can still be heard but they now seem to belong to another world, from which one appears to be cut off. And yet one isn't, for at the end of each alley houses or trees are visible, and the paths, made up of eight rows of small square flagstones laid on rubble and earth with the divisions between the stones clearly demarcated, accentuate the straightness, as in a demonstration of classical perspective. At the same time the undulation of the ground means that the open ends always seem the same distance away, which leads to a sense of unreality, of something both firmly physical and yet utterly dreamlike. Eisenman has described it as 'an ordered system which has lost touch with human reason', but, like all such statements by artists about their work, it is at best partial and at worst misleading. It may be that this is what he wanted to convey, but fortunately what he has made is bigger, more complex and more resistant to meaning than his summary implies.

It is not without significance that Eisenman was originally going to work with Richard Serra, though the sculptor withdrew at a fairly early stage, insisting that this was not for ideological reasons but simply because of the pressure of other commitments. Yet the Memorial has all the hallmarks of Serra's work. In them, as Rosalind Kraus has well brought out in a brilliant essay on the sculptor's work, his aim is to ask us not to *see* but to *experience*. We are asked to use our bodies to enter and move about a work like *Shift*, an immense sculpture that spans nearly three hundred metres in rural Canada, and our response to it is pre-verbal and pre-visual, 'pre-objective', as Kraus puts it. This is a world where you *feel* rather than *see* your way, since obstacles to an unimpeded view are constantly arising. For it is the body, as Kraus points out, that is the pre-objective ground of all experience.[31] In keeping with this, the Berlin Memorial is made out of the most uninteresting of materials, concrete, at once long-lasting and ephemeral, grey, colourless, an aid to construction rather than anything in itself, and thus the absolute opposite of marble, that quintessential material of Renaissance monumental sculpture, which asks to be looked at and admired. The Memorial's concrete blocks emphatically do not ask to be looked at, we are barely aware of them except as parts of a whole which cannot quite be taken in, which is in a sense both utterly there and not quite there, both an invitation and a barrier.

As one might have expected of a project of such huge symbolic significance, the Berlin Holocaust Memorial was dogged by controversy from the start. An earlier competition, as Carrier points out, was aborted when the then Chancellor, Helmut Kohl, who had long been a champion of such a memorial, objected to the original shortlisted entries. Soon after Eisenman and Serra had won the second competition the sculptor withdrew; and after the monument had been completed (Eisenman was forced to reduce the stelae from the originally envisaged 4000 to 2,700 and to make a number

---

31 Rosalind Kraus, 'Richard Serra, a Translation', in *The Originality of the Avant-Garde and Other Modernist Myths* (Cambridge, Mass.; 1986).

of other adjustments), there was felt to be a danger that neo-Nazi groups would daub the blocks with graffiti. The company employed to do the work of covering them with a special anti-graffiti coating was then accused by the Swiss of having once had Nazi links, but the controversy died away when it was revealed that a Swiss firm had put in a bid for the coating but had lost out. By then, though, there had been plenty of voices objecting to this or that aspect of the monument or to the whole idea of such a memorial. Some objected to a memorial solely for Jewish victims, while the President of the Central Council for Jews in Germany criticised it for providing no information on Nazi perpetrators and therefore blunting the visitors' confrontation with the crime. In answer to the first criticism one might reply that the fact that this memorial commemorates the Jewish victims does not preclude other monuments being erected in the future to other victims. In answer to the second one could argue that Germany and Berlin in particular, is full of sites where hugely detailed information is provided concerning the perpetrators, the most striking perhaps being the villa on the lake at Wannsee where at a conference in 1942 the plans for the Final Solution were thrashed out. No-one could accuse the Germans of trying to hide their dreadful past. Nevertheless, in response to this charge, Eisenman agreed to build an adjacent, mainly underground information centre next to the monument, though in no way impinging on it.

More telling has been the criticism of certain German writers and intellectuals. When the project was first mooted Günter Grass called for it to be abandoned. When it was unveiled Martin Walser, accepting the Peace Prize of the German book trade, used the opportunity to decry 'the exploitation of our disgrace for present purposes', and criticised the 'monumentalisation and ceaseless presentation of our shame', which, he felt, was rife in Germany at the time.

'Auschwitz,' he concluded, 'is not suitable for becoming... an always available intimidation or a moral club, or just an obligation. What is produced by ritualization has the quality of mere lip service.'

Of course, there is always the danger of 'the exploitation of... disgrace for present purposes'. We have seen many examples of this in the course of this book. My own feeling is that Auschwitz itself should not be, as it has become, a place of ritual pilgrimage. But the power of the Serra/Eisenman/Hoppold Berlin Memorial lies, to my mind, precisely in its reticence. As Eisenman and Serra would have it, it is designed to evoke 'a new idea of memory' by commemorating the past without recourse to symbols. The visitor is free to visit the information centre or not. The blocks and the way they are laid out may remind some of cemeteries and others of the nightmare of Nazi persecutions or of history, but they leave a space for children to play and families to visit and individuals to wander and – yes – to get temporarily and frighteningly lost in. They are simply there, neither a blot on the skyline nor a call to solemnity, just 2,700 concrete blocks laid on subtly and imperceptibly shifting ground, a trigger for memory or meditation, a space to explore, in which normal life can be suspended for as long or short a time as you like.

*

It is interesting to compare it to two other public monuments, Rachel Whiteread's Judenplatz memorial to the murdered Jews of Austria and the 9/11 monument in New York.

Rachel Whiteread's memorial stands in a small bare square in the central district of Vienna, which was in the Middle Ages the centre of a bustling Jewish life and the scene of a pogrom in which a hundred Jews were burned. It consists of a steel and concrete construction with a base ten by seven metres and a height of 3.6 metres. The artist calls it a Nameless Library, and the conceit is that this is the cast of a modestly sized room lined with books, the walls of which have been removed, leaving us with shelves of books whose spines face inwards, away from us, and are thus not visible. The shelves appear to hold endless copies of the same book. There are no windows and the double doors are cast with the panels inside out and have no doorknobs or handles.

The memorial could not be more different from its Berlin counterpart. Where that was immense yet blurred the boundaries between inner and outer, monument and city, this is small, closed off, austere. Most strikingly, it is on a plinth, separated from even the small silent square (very different from the constant hum of traffic and pedestrians that surrounds the Berlin monument) as decisively as any nineteenth century monument. Like all of Whiteread's work, though, it is both solidly 'there', like the Arc de Triomphe, and puzzlingly elusive.

Whiteread has always been concerned with a central paradox. She wants to depict the evanescent, the ordinary, even, as Georges Perec would put it, the 'infra-ordinary', with mattresses, hot-water bottles, tables, chairs, cupboards – all the drab furnishings of ordinary households – as signs of the humdrum lives of which they are a part and which could not function, in modern Western societies, without them. But she wants to do so in a way that both stresses their ephemeral nature and monumentalises them. Her first major work was the cast of a room in a house in North London that was about to be demolished, and she titled it *Ghost*. This has led some to talk about the role of nostalgia in her work, the (very English) evocation of a vanishing past. But I think her work is much stranger than that implies, and takes her much closer to someone like Rilke, say, who was concerned in all his work with giving us the sense of the mysterious *otherness* of the world, or of Perec, whose work is similarly orientated, though in a less solemn, lighter way. She has talked about how, in the midst of working on *Ghost*, immured in that room and spraying it with plaster, she had a moment of revelation where she felt herself to be no longer a human being but one of the walls of the room. By this I don't think she meant a mere onlooker onto the vanished life of the room but rather that she had shed her private concerns, even her humanity, and become one with the structure. On first acquaintance with her work we may reach for what seems most accessible about it and call it evocative or nostalgic, but in fact, like Cézanne's, it is as tough as nails – and as enigmatic.

The paradox lies in the fact that by making a cast of a hot-water bottle, a bathtub, the space under a chair or a whole house, she turns the space which an evanescent object has occupied into something hard and the unchanging. For earlier monument-builders and statue-makers the purpose of their work was to make something that would, by its hardness and monumentality, keep something that had once been alive from ever dyng. They felt, as did their subjects and those who commissioned them, that by turning Admiral Nelson or General Gordon into a statue they had, in a sense, fulfilled that subject's potential, which was to rise above the merely human and assume heroic, even godlike proportions. But what if you no longer believe this? What if you believe that what is important about human beings is nothing other than their embeddedness in their daily humdrum activities, that what makes us human is precisely that ordinariness, that vulnerability and mortality, and that it is this that needs to be rendered? Then you are forced to recognise that by giving permanence to this you are in effect destroying what you set out to create.

That has been the dilemma of modern art from its beginnings, with Cézanne, with Proust, with Virginia Woolf, with Bonnard, with Rilke. And each great modern artist has resolved the problem in his or her own way. Whiteread's way is to heighten the sense of paradox in order to force us to recognise the gulf that exists between the evanescence of life and the solidity of art. *Ghost* is anything but ghostly. Her materials are plaster and concrete, not gauze. It would have been easy to create a replica of that room and exhibit it, but she has chosen to fill the space so that no ghost can walk and we cannot penetrate, only scrabble in vain around the periphery. That is why critics have such difficulty with her work, for anything one says about it immediately turns it into an object for our contemplation instead of a paradox to be wrestled with.

Think now about books. The printed book as it emerged in the fifteenth and sixteenth centuries is an object, like its medieval predecessor, the manuscript book. It is of course a less expensive and prestigious object because it is infinitely repeatable. That, indeed, is what is so wonderful about it: the same book can be reproduced as often as required, giving it the sense of being more of a thing, an object that is part and parcel of life, than its predecessor, which was seen as a precious possession available only to the very wealthy. Yet what the printed book contains in its pages is not any *thing*, it is an invitation to a kind of dialogue. You pick up a book and start to read, which means that you lose a sense of where you are and what precisely it is you are holding and engage with what it is saying to you. But that makes it a profoundly paradoxical object, as paradoxical as Hamlet's recorder – a piece of wood and yet for those who can play it something that brings forth sweet music that belongs to another world than wood or fingers. As paradoxical too as human beings, who are solid objects that cast shadows but who, once we get to know them, are infinitely more and other than that.

Renaissance writes like Rabelais and Cervantes and, after them, Swift and Sterne, were fascinated by this double aspect of the printed book. They understood how easy and how dangerous it was to imagine that because they were objects they could be fully understood, and they relished the fact that books will always frustrate those who try to prise out their secrets, like Rosencrantz and Guildenstern with Hamlet. That is the dangerous fantasy, Swift suggests in *A Tale of a Tub*, of both Catholic and Protestant zealots who torture the Bible in order to tease out of it the meaning they wish to find. But, these writers argue, books are like people, and if we wish to engage with them we have to enter into dialogue with them and we have to accept that we will never know them completely.

Thus Rachel Whiteread's monument to the dead Jews of Austria, her Nameless Library, works with a double paradox: the paradox of making solid what was living and evanescent in order to commemorate the living and evanescent, and the paradox of celebrating books, more central to the lives of Jews than any other people, by turning them into concrete.

'My works are very much concerned with the body and with human touch,' Whiteread has said. 'Whether it's my touch or someone else's or a whole family's touch, they are about [an object] that has been used.' Yet unlike the Berlin Memorial, which asks us to wander through the labyrinth and experience in our moving bodies the sense of disorientation it induces, it stands on its plinth, foursquare, utterly impenetrable. But that sense of impenetrability, of our being unable to get at these books, at the people who used these books, is itself a powerful experience, is itself, I would argue, the experience of the monument. We want to get closer – and we can't. That sense of distance felt on our bodies just as much as in the Berlin monument brings us into dialogue with it and brings with it a powerful sense of other lives, of the mystery of their existence and of the utter sadness not just of what happened to these people but also of what inevitably happens to all our dead and, of course, what will happen to us. And even more than the Berlin monument, it does this with a serenity we might be tempted to call classical.

As with its Berlin counterpart the genesis of the Nameless Library was fraught with problems, and it has also been the subject of much criticism. The project was championed by Simon Wiesenthal, the renowned Nazi hunter, who had become the spokesman of those who had been offended by an earlier, quite realistic memorial, 'Against War and Fascism', by Alfred Hrdlicka in the Albertinaplatz. Whiteread's design for a new monument was unanimously chosen by an international jury, but though it had been due to be inaugurated on 9 November 1996, the fifty-eighth anniversary of Kristallnacht, it was delayed by four years due to political and aesthetic controversies. Most crucial of all was an objection by the Jewish authorities that building it in the Judenplatz would endanger the archaeological site of the medieval Jewish synagogue which lay beneath. Eventually, though, all these matters were resolved.

Rachel Whiteread surely intended the starkness and simplicity of the monument to stand in deliberate contrast to the elaborate Baroque art and architecture of Vienna. A member of the jury suggested a resemblance to a bunker and the artist herself later confirmed that the German military fortifications of the Atlantic Wall, which she visited as part of her research, had been a source of inspiration. Some have felt that it was intended to reveal the tragedy and brutality of the Holocaust, a notion given prominence by Simon Wiesenthal at the unveiling when he said: 'The Monument shouldn't be beautiful. It must hurt.' But as with the Berlin monument its success is due precisely to its reticence, its refusal to make 'a statement'. It is a striking work which makes an immediate impression, standing as it does quite alone in the empty little square surrounded by tall handsome houses, but it is up to the visitor to decide whether it asserts the dignity of the People of the Book or the horror of their annihilation. Indeed, its strength lies precisely in the fact that it can evoke one feeling one day and another the next, and often several feelings at once. It calls us into dialogue with it, with ourselves, with the clouds in the sky above. That, today, with so fraught a subject for commemoration, is quite an achievement.

*

On 11 September 2011, on the tenth anniversary of the attacks that destroyed the Twin Towers of the World Trade Centre in Lower Manhattan, the official memorial to those who died in the attack was dedicated at Ground Zero. Designed by Michael Arad and the landscape architect Peter Walker, it was given the title 'Reflecting Absence'. Just under thirty-two and a half thousand square metres in size, it consists of two sunken reflecting pools, each surrounded by an enormous waterfall The names of the 2,983 people who died in the attacks as well as those who died in the failed attempt to destroy the towers in 1993 are etched in bronze panels which edge the ponds. A lengthy Mission Statement forms part of the Memorial. It concludes: 'May the lives be remembered, the deeds recognised, and the spirit reawakened by eternal beacons, which reaffirm respect for life, strengthen our resolve to preserve freedom, and inspire an end to hatred, ignorance and intolerance.'

This rousing message is surely a mistake. Rieff, in *In Praise of Forgetting*, makes the point forcefully:

> Although there is nothing morally problematic about remembering the fallen and honouring the heroism of the first responders, the call to 'strengthen our resolve to preserve freedom' is anything but an innocent piety. To the contrary, it bears echoes of President George W. Bush's speech to a joint session of Congress nine days after the attacks, in which he argued that

they had occurred because the terrorists 'hate our freedoms – our freedom of religion, our freedom of speech, our freedom to vote and assemble and disagree with each other'. (128)

'Even those who have accepted Bush's account,' he goes on, 'despite its failure to acknowledge the possibility that it was America's actions globally rather than the American way of life that the jihadis hated, presumably would grant that the President was making a political claim.' Such claims, however disguised, should have no place on a memorial, private or public. At the same time the title of the Memorial, 'Reflecting Absence', seems to me to be an attempt to push the visitor into thinking along certain lines. All memorials, after all, 'reflect absence', but the best of them, I have been suggesting, create a space in which the visitor or passer-by is encouraged to step outside the daily treadmill and look and ponder – or not, if he or she does not feel like it. When the traditional way of doing these things is no longer taken for granted the best policy should be to say as little as possible and to let the monument speak for itself, as do the Berlin and Vienna Holocaust Memorials. To try to do more is to fall into the trap Sterne alerted us to more than two and a half centuries ago: by trying to nudge the viewer into experiencing a particular set of feelings you destroy the delicate balance between the viewer and the work.

'In shouldering the memory-work, monuments may relieve viewers of their memory burden', remarks Young disapprovingly, but, as I have been arguing, the more it shoulders the memory burden the better the monument does its job. To live day in day out with such a burden is debilitating for both society and the individual. By shouldering the burden the monument relieves us of the need to remember all the time, allows us to forget. For only he who forgets remembers.

Interlude

I EXAMINE A PHOTOGRAPH IN THE
NEWSPAPER[32]

It takes time to read an image.

My eye caught by a grimy little black and white photo in
the top right-hand corner of the page, I spread the paper flat
on my desk and lean over it to try and get a better view.

What I first see is a woman standing in a wood in the
sunlight. It seems to be spring or early summer, for the leaves
are out, though not so thickly as to hide the branches, the
trunks. The woman is young and sturdy and, from what I
can make out, rather beautiful. She stands sideways to the
camera, looking off to the right, her features hidden by her
abundant glossy hair, cropped at the shoulders. Next to her is
the misshapen trunk of a large tree whose branches are cut off
by the top edge of the photo, a black mass filling the right-
hand side.

The sunlight plays on the woman's back as she stands
looking off to the right. A sense of peace pervades the scene.

What is she looking at? Her right arm hangs at her side yet
her hand is held slightly away from her and her fist appears
to be clenched, though it is difficult to see clearly as a leafy
sapling half hides it. She is wearing a sweater of some light
colour and a white skirt, smooth around the buttocks, pleated
below, which barely reaches to her knees. The light catches
the backs of her strong shapely legs and her bare feet, the left
half hidden by the right. Her heels are slightly higher than her

---

32 Reprinted from *Heart's Wings and Other Stories* (Carcanet, 2010).

toes, though she does not appear to be straining as she would be were she standing on tiptoe.

Some images exude noise, activity, others stillness, silence. Here the sense is of utter silence in the forest, utter peace, with only the sunlight, the trees and the solitary woman.

Beneath her feet, more leaves. Yet she does not appear to be standing on a bed of leaves. In fact, as I look more closely, I see that there is a small but distinct gap between her feet and the floor of the forest.

And then suddenly I understand what it is I am looking at and my stomach turns. The woman is not standing at all. She is hanging from a branch of the dark misshapen tree, though the rope from which she hangs is lost in the sunlight, the leaves and the branches, while her abundant glossy hair hides the noose about her neck.

Now that I understand what it is I am seeing I can sense how the body would move, turning a little this way and that in the breeze, if there is any breeze in this silent, sunlit wood.

Only then do I read the caption: 'A refugee from Srebrenica who hanged herself after the Serb capture of the city.'

X

THE BURIAL OF THE DEAD (2)

Humans bury their dead in order to ensure a proper separation between the living and the dead. They bury them with due ceremony in order both to remember and to forget. The horror of the unburied spirit who has found no resting-place and comes back to haunt the living has been a feature of the human imagination from the earliest times and is vividly conveyed in the stories of Elpenor in the *Odyssey* and Palinurus in the *Aeneid*. Unburied, they still haunt their living comrades and will continue to do so until their bodies are found and put in the earth with due form.

But there is never any doubt that proper burial is possible. The extraordinary power of *Hamlet* as a transitional text, standing at the point, 1600, when the old ways were starting to disappear and new ones beginning to emerge is nowhere more evident than in the prominence it gives to a ghost who haunts the living yet can never be properly laid to rest. It is striking too that not one of the exceedingly large number who die in the course of the play receives proper burial.

The play, at its simplest, is about whether it is possible for Old Hamlet to be put back in the earth in such a way that he will not walk on it again. And the answer seems to be that it is not. The plot gets under way because he cannot rest in his grave and returns to haunt the battlements of Elsinore dressed in a full suit of armour. By the end of Act I we know the reason why and we seem to know how something may be done about it: he has been falsely given out as having died in his sleep whereas he was in fact murdered by his brother, and he will find rest again only when he is avenged by his son. But by the end of the play we understand that though this may be the way things look to him, it is not (quite) the way it looks to the son. In the course of the playing out of the mismatch between the expectations of the father and the possibilities presented to the son, the old court councillor Polonius is killed and his corpse goes missing. When it is found it is secretly buried, the reason given by the king being that to make it public would be to provoke an uprising among his subjects. However, this does not satisfy Polonius's own son, Laertes, who bursts into the presence of the king with a simple request: 'Give me my father.' When Claudius promises to explain who killed his father and how, and assures him that he will help him seek revenge, Laertes is only partially pacified:

> Let this be so.
> His means of death, his obscure funeral –
> No trophy, sword or hatchment o'er his bones,
> No noble rite, nor formal ostentation –
> Cry to be heard as 'twere from heaven to earth
> That I must call't in question. (4.5.303–8, Arden 3, B text)

(Harold Jenkins, the editor of the Arden 2 *Hamlet*, glosses 'hatchment' as 'a tablet or painting displaying the coat-of-arms of the deceased, normally placed outside the house of mourning, and then, after the burial, over the tomb.')

In between Laertes' first demand and this passage, though, we have had sight of his sister, Ophelia, now mad – though whether driven to this by her father's death or Hamlet's rejection of her or by the recognition that the man she loved has killed her father, or all three, the play leaves us to decide. Suffice it to say that while Hamlet feigned madness, often rather impressively, the real thing, present before us on the stage, leaves us frightened and bewildered. That is because madness, like Alzheimer's, brings us face to face with a person who seems in many ways unchanged except that now they have stepped outside the norms of humanity in the way they speak, the things they say and even the clothes they wear. And the combination of the two things is heart-rending to witness. For here is someone like us, and yet in some crucial ways no longer like us at all. Very like a ghost in fact.

Soon, of course, it will be Ophelia's grave that Laertes will leap into, furious at what the priest officiating at her funeral says to him as he explains the official attitude of the Church towards one who has taken her own life. 'What ceremony else?' Laertes asks, implying that he is dissatisfied with what the priest has so far told him about the form her burial will take. The man explains:

> Her obsequies have been so far enlarged
> As we have warranty. Her death was doubtful,
> And but that great command o'ersways the order
> She should in ground unsanctified been lodged
> Till the last trumpet: for charitable prayers,
> Flints and pebbles would be thrown on her.
> Yet here she is allowed her virgin crants,
> Her maiden strewments, and the bringing home
> Of bell and burial. (5.1.215–22. Arden 3, B text)

(Jenkins glosses 'crants' as a 'garland worn as a sign of maidenhood, placed on the bier at burial and afterwards hung up in church.')

Laertes can't believe his ears. 'Must there no more be done?' he asks again. 'No more be done,' responds he priest:

> We should profane the service of the dead
> To sing a requiem and such rest to her
> As to peace-parted souls.

But this is, finally, too much for Laertes:

> Lay her I'th'earth,
> And from her fair and unpolluted flesh
> May violets spring. I tell thee, churlish priest,
> A ministering angel shall my sister be
> When thou liest howling. (224–30)

It is at this point that Hamlet, who, with Horatio, has been watching unobserved, grasps who it is who is being buried. His words, 'What? The fair Ophelia?' overshadow, for the audience, the words his mother then speaks over Ophelia's grave:

> Sweets to the sweet, farewell.
> I had hoped thou should'st have been my Hamlet's wife;
> I thought thy bride-bed to have decked, sweet maid,
> And not have strewed thy grave. (231–5)

We never actually find out how Ophelia is eventually buried, for at this moment Laertes leaps into the grave with a mighty Marlovian rant: 'Hold off the earth awhile, / Till I have caught her once more in my arms,' to be followed by Hamlet's own echoing vaunt: 'This is I, / Hamlet the Dane.' By the time order has been restored and Hamlet has left the scene with 'I loved you ever – but it is no matter', followed by the faithful Horatio, and Claudius has managed to reassure Laertes that he will help him find revenge, Ophelia is forgotten.

What follows, of course, is a veritable avalanche of deaths, and, as the unburied dead strew the stage and Hamlet himself expires, Fortinbras, the Norwegian prince, arrives, just in time to take over the rotten state of Denmark. 'Where is the sight?' he exclaims as he surveys the scene. The editors of the most recent Arden edition of the play gloss this by saying:

'Fortinbras has apparently been warned what to expect', implying that he is looking round for the bodies. But this is surely much too weak. The bodies of Gertrude, Claudius and the expiring Hamlet and Laertes, for one thing, are surely prominent, not hidden away in some corner of the stage, requiring Fortinbras to peer round and ask where they are. And why should Shakespeare opt for so banal an opening to his climactic scene? Surely it is better to take the words as a reference to the Apocalypse. Fortinbras would then be saying: 'Surely we are no longer on earth as we have always known it; we are witnessing the End of Days.' Then, in keeping with his military and political mindset, he quickly stakes his claim:

> With sorrow I embrace my fortune.
> I have some rights of memory in this kingdom
> Which now I claim my vantage doth invite me. (372–4)

Having made that clear, he turns again to the scene before him:

> Let four captains
> Bear Hamlet like a soldier to the stage,
> For he was likely, had he been put on [given the opportunity]
> To have proved most royal. And for this passage
> The soldiers' music and the rite of war
> Speak loudly for him.
> Take up the bodies. Such a sight as this
> Becomes the field but here shows much amiss.
> Go bid the soldiers shoot. (779–87)

So a play which opened with a restless ghost haunting the living ends not with its proper burial and not even with the proper burial of the hero, as happens at the end of the *Iliad* and *Beowulf*, but with a projected burial, while the remaining

123

dead are unceremoniously dragged away to clear the stage for the entire cast to return to take their bows, a resurrection which only the theatre can provide.

*

Hamlet was prescient. Our modern world is haunted by hauntings, from the Gothic novels of the eighteenth century to the popular novels of the Victorians and the short stories of M.R. James to the many memorable filmic hauntings with which Hollywood has enthralled and terrified us for the past hundred years. I want to conclude, though, not with any of these but with a beautiful example from an author not usually associated with the ghost story, Franz Kafka.

A boat arrives in the harbour of the north Italian town of Riva.[33] Two men in dark coats with silver buttons carry a bier ashore, accompanied by the pilot, who asks the way and is directed to a house in the town. Having taken the bier there they set it down in an upstairs room, then light candles at its head. On the bier lies a man with wildly matted hair. A gentleman in a top hat, who turns out to be the burgomaster of the town, has meanwhile arrived, knelt down beside the bier and started to pray. The pilot motions to the bearers to leave and they do so, but then the kneeling man nods to him and he too departs.

A strange conversation now ensues between the top-hatted Burgomaster and the man on the bier. 'You probably know that I am the Hunter Gracchus', the man says. 'Certainly,' responds the Burgomaster. 'Your arrival was announced to me during the night.' He goes on to explain that a huge dove had

---

33 Franz Kafka, 'The Hunter Gracchus'. I use the translation by Willa and Edwin Muir, slightly modified, but there are by now multiple translations in print.

flown in at his window and said in his ear: 'Tomorrow the dead Hunter Gracchus is coming: receive him in the name of the city.' Yes, nods the hunter, the doves flew ahead of me. 'But do you believe, Burgomaster, that I shall remain in Riva?' 'I cannot say,' responds the other. 'Are you dead?'

'Yes,' said the hunter, 'as you see. Many years ago, yes, it must be a great many years ago, I fell from a precipice in the Black Forest – that is in Germany – when I was hunting chamois. Since then I have been dead.'

'But you are alive too,' said the Burgomaster.

'In a certain sense,' said the hunter. 'In a certain sense I am alive too. My death ship lost its way; a wrong turn of the wheel, a moment's absence of mind on the pilot's part, a longing to turn aside towards my lovely native country. I cannot tell what it was; I only know this, that I remained on earth and that ever since my ship has sailed earthly waters.'

'Extraordinary,' says the Burgomaster when the hunter has finished his account (which goes on for several pages). 'And now,' he adds, 'do you think of staying here with us?'

'I think not', said the hunter with a smile, and, to excuse himself, he laid his hand on the Burgomaster's knee. 'I am here, more than that I do not know, further than that I cannot go. My ship has no rudder, and it is driven by the wind that blows in the nethermost regions of death.'

*

Is our modern fear of forgetting linked in some way to our inability to bury the dead? We bury them all right, of course, but does such burial mean very much, do we inhabit the rites we perform on these occasions in such a way as really to ensure a separation between us and the dead? And without such a separation without an acceptance on our part that the dead will not return to us but that we will go to them, can they really be laid to rest? And if it is indeed the case, as Beckett said and as Proust showed, that only he who forgets remembers, then do we have to accept that in a sense we today, as Nietzsche argued, can neither forget nor remember, neither sleep properly nor be properly awake? Kafka certainly felt this and lamented, in his diaries that because he did not feel really alive he feared he could not really die. 'The Hunter Gracchus' is the fruit of such feelings. It is one we have surely all shared at one time or another. None of us, of course, has been able to express it so resonantly.

XI

HAUNTINGS

What are the roots that clutch, what branches grow
Out of this stony rubbish? Son of man
You cannot say, or guess, for you know only
A heap of broken images, here the sun beats,
And the dead tree gives no shelter, the cricket no relief,
And the dry stone no sound of water.

This is Eliot's waste land, a spiritual as well as a physical state
in the immediate aftermath of the First World War. Though
he struggled for a long time to find the right epigraph for
the poem, which remained even after Pound's ministrations,
as strange to him as it was – and remains – to his readers
(though he and most of them sensed at once that it was a
major poem), he did in the end find the perfect thing. It is
a quote from Petronius, the second-century Latin writer, a
precursor of Rabelais or Thomas Bernhard, and it goes: 'I
saw with my own eyes the Sybil of Cumae hanging in a jar,
and when the boys said to her: Sybil, what do you wish for?'
she answered them: 'I wish to die.' Or, in the original, which
is what Eliot places at the top of his poem: 'Nam Sybillam
quidem Cumis ego ipse oculis meis vidi in ampulla pendere,
et cum illi pueri dicerent: "Sibylla, ti theleis?" respondebat illa:
"Apothanein thelo.'"The boys' question and the Sybil's answer
are in Greek and written in Greek characters, thus making the
whole passage even more impenetrable to a modern reader
without a classical education. But this is not an example of
elitism on Eliot's part, or of disdain for his reader, but rather
one example with which he presents us, right here at the

start, of our distance from the past, our inability to speak and understand its languages; which is, after all, one of the central themes of the poem. For us in the waste land, he is saying – and demonstrating – there is only a heap of broken images, no shelter from the unbearable sun and not even the sound of water – only these strange words in strange languages which can never, for that reason, allay our thirst. We must hold this in mind – or perhaps accept the experience would be a better way of putting it – to grasp that even though we now have found a translation we cannot simply proceed with our reading of the poem. That is to misread Eliot at the very start. As Hugh Kenner, Eliot's best critic, once put it, the fact that the epigraph is there, not what it means, is what is important.[34]

Because we cannot properly remember, because our culture has cut us off from the past but put nothing in its place, we cannot properly forget. Like the Sybil, we sit hunched in our little bubble (*ampulla*) and we want, if this is all the world has to offer us, to die; but we can't.

In the unreal city the crowds flow over London Bridge like the spirits in Dante's limbo, but also like Kafka's Hunter Gracchus, not fully alive and not fully dead. There, says the narrator:

> I saw one I knew, and stopped him, crying: 'Stetson!
> You who were with me in the ships at Mylae!
> That corpse you planted last year in your garden,
> Has it begun to sprout? Will it bloom this year?
> Or has the sudden frost disturbed its bed?
> Oh Keep the Dog far hence, that's friend to men,
> Or with his nails he'll dig it up again!

---

34   Hugh Kenner, *The Invisible Poet: T.S. Eliot* (London; 1965), p.43.

We all have corpses buried somewhere in our garden, corpses we are afraid to think about, corpses which will not remain safely buried, which we are afraid will bloom like hothouse plants which the dog will one day dig up. This is the condition of the waste land of modernity, that we no longer know how to bury our dead so that they stay buried. Instead we try to shut out all thought of them. Burial would allow for a proper separation of body and spirit and allow the spirit of the dead to watch over us and help us live our lives. It would also allow us to accept that one day we too must join them. The denial of death and of the dead, on the other hand, means that we live in a perpetual state of anxiety, ready to do anything to stop ourselves thinking of what is there in the garden and what awaits us in the end. Such a situation is a nightmare from which we are for ever trying to awake, but in vain: we are in the waste land and there is no exit.

But while that may be what the poem, especially in its early stages, *says*, it is not quite what it *does*; what it does to the reader, to us as we read. For though the land is still waste and arid at the end something, because of what we have been through, because of what Eliot has enticed us into facing up to (even if we hardly recognise it), has begun to change:

> Ganga was sunken, and the limp leaves
> Waited for rain while the black clouds
> Gathered far distant, over Himavant.
> The jungle crouched, humped in silence.
> Then spoke the thunder.

The limp leaves sense that rain is on the way, and the thunder heralds it. This time, unlike with the words of Petronius in the epigraph, there is no difficulty in understanding it, for it speaks in a universal language, one which is never forgotten. Our sense of excitement as we read the poem and of growing anticipation as we move towards its conclusion is due to the fact that our immersion in the world of the waste land was a necessary prelude to its transformation. Without the one, not even the possibility of the other. To read much of the night and go south in winter to escape the cold or have a furtive sexual encounter in a bedsitter may keep thoughts of the buried corpse at bay, but they will lead to no transformation.

The thunder is unforgiving. It says: 'The awful daring of a moment's surrender / Which an age of prudence can never retract. / By this, and this only, we have existed.' It sounds again, and this time: 'I have heard the key / Turn in the door once and once only. / We think of the key, each in his prison.' But by the third roll of thunder something has changed: 'The boat responded / Gaily, to the hand expert with sail and oar.' And then the end comes rushing on, but this time instead of being overwhelmed by a heap of broken images, the speaker takes responsibility: 'These fragments I have shored against my ruins.' And at the very end there is only the calm breathing of the Sanskrit words, as far as it is possible to get from the anguished incomprehensibility of 'ti theleis' and 'apothanein thelo':

> Datta. Dayadhvam. Damyata.
> Shantih shantih shantih

Hugh Kenner, still the sharpest of Eliot's readers, tacitly correcting the poet's later remark that the poem was written 'in a fit of pique', likened *The Waste Land* to a prolonged bout of pins and needles. The analogy is accurate. The pain and discomfort we feel when we get pins and needles is due to the fact that the blood is once again coursing in a limb that had grown numb. Without the discomfort there would be no chance of restoring it to a healthy functioning state. In the modern world, in which the rituals of burial and mourning have been lost, and especially in the aftermath of the slaughter of World War I, which swept away all structures of meaning and authority, it is art that has taken their place. Like the burial ritual, the modern work of art, if it is to be true to its condition, will have to enact the mourning and then the acceptance of guilt (there is always guilt for the survivor) and loss. Only when we have followed it down into the depths can we get a glimpse of the stars, a sense of the possible rain to come. Anything more would falsify the way things are and render its consolations ineffective.

*

A few novelists, like the best poets, have grasped this. In what is one of Muriel Spark's most perfect and profound books, *Memento Mori*, a group of old people is plagued by a mysterious voice on the phone which says only one thing to them: 'Remember you must die.' One of the victims is Dame Lettie Coulson, 'seventy-nine lifelong committee woman and organiser of good causes'. For her, fit and active as she still is, 'there is no such thing as old age'. On a visit to Jean Taylor, once her sister-in-law's maid and now living in an old people's home, she asks: 'What should I do about the phone calls?'

> 'Can you not ignore it, Dame Lettie?'
> 'No. I cannot. I have tried, but it troubles me deeply. It is a troublesome remark.'
> 'Perhaps you might obey it,' said Miss Taylor.
> 'What's that you say?'
> 'You might perhaps try to remember you must die.'
> She is wandering again, thought Lettie. 'Taylor, she said, 'I do not wish to be advised how to think.'

Spark returns to this in a later novel, *The Hothouse by the East River*. We are now in New York, where the radiators burn and people seem to lead their lives as in a dream. The book opens in a shoe shop with Elsa trying on a pair of shoes. Suddenly she has the impression that the salesman who is helping her is someone she had once known. She hurries out. Everywhere she goes people are startled by the fact that she casts her shadow in the opposite way to everyone else. Gradually the figures in her past gather and the mystery is explained. Elsa and her husband had died many years before, in a train accident. They have, in a sense, only been kept conscious by their visceral determination to deny death. But here too the law holds that if you deny him Death will eventually remind you of his presence. The novel itself thus comes to be seen as the result of such an effort of the will and the imagination, so that its end signals the final release of those desperate souls into a kind of peace, the final succumbing of the fevered imagination to the dictates of reality.

William Golding's *Pincher Martin* could not be more different from these Spark novels, but it explores the same theme. The eponymous protagonist, belying his given name of Christopher (the Christ-bearer), has been deeply selfish all his life, a man who does not recognise other people except as ladders or obstacles to his self-fulfilment. Now, shipwrecked on a rock in the middle of the ocean, he fights off the thought that the only thing that has ever mattered to him, himself, is about to disappear for ever. The novel seems to be entering *Robinson Crusoe* territory as Martin starts to reconnoitre the tiny island and work out how he can survive till he is rescued. But here too the moral holds that if you try to forget that death exists it will remind you of its presence. The contours of the island have for some time been feeling strangely familiar to Martin, though he cannot put his finger on the reason for this. Suddenly in one of those dizzying moments for both protagonist and reader which makes those early Golding novels so remarkable, it hits him that the rock he thought he had been climbing over for the past few days has precisely the contours of one of his own teeth over which his tongue has been sliding. What he had thought was out there in the world is suddenly revealed to be only the projection of his fevered imagination as it struggles to maintain itself. The shattering effect of this discovery on the reader as well as the protagonist stems from the fact that we have been doing our own readerly work of conjuring a whole solid world out of the protagonist's imaginings. But that in turn only exists because it has been imagined by the novelist. In this way Golding, like Spark, turns the novel against itself to reveal why it is we cling so desperately to ourselves when we know, deep down, that one day we will have to let go.

XII

LETTING GO

We have seen how profoundly intertwined are memory and forgetting and we have tracked the modern fear of forgetting down to its lair: the fear of the final forgetting, what Raymond Chandler called The Big Sleep.

But if art leads us there it is only in order to allay that fear. Not totally, of course, no one would be foolish enough to imagine that was possible. But, by making it known, to make it less potent. And that means helping us to let go – to let go of the world, let go of ourselves. Not (unless you are a Buddhist) because the world does not really exist, but because sooner or later a letting go will anyway take place, whether we like it or not. And nothing I know more movingly explores this than the late poems of Wallace Stevens, which are to all extents and purposes an extended farewell to the world he had loved so much and celebrated so ardently.

They are the poems of an old man who, as he dramatises himself in some of them, is often asleep or half-asleep, and in one is a child asleep, 'in its own dreams'. Sometimes there is the suggestion that the sleeper was never really awake:

You were not born yet when the trees were crystal
Nor are you now, in this wakefulness inside a sleep. (443)[35]

---

35 I use the Library of America edition of the *Collected Poetry and Prose*, edited by Frank Kermode and Joan Richardson (1997).

Sometimes, as in 'The Sick Man', he lies in bed, listening, waiting imagining. But mostly he is half-asleep, on the threshold between two worlds, like his old friend and mentor George Santayana in the monastery in Rome where he has retired to die:

> Your dozing in the depths of wakefulness,
> In the warmth of your bed, at the edge of your chair alive
> Yet living in two worlds...
> Impatient for the grandeur that you need
> In so much misery. (433)

The 'misery' is what he elsewhere calls 'poverty', and both words come to have more positive associations for Stevens as he ages, signifying a stripping down to essentials, while 'grandeur' is the sense of fulfilment, of finally coming home to where you really belong. This had always been Stevens' secret goal, what he had always instinctively felt that only the writing of poetry would help him reach. What is new here is the sense of time running out and of the radical reduction of life's possibilities which, paradoxically, brings him closer to his goal than he had ever been as all that is inessential is stripped away:

> It is poverty's speech that seeks us out the most.
> It is older than the oldest speech of Rome.
> This is the tragic accent of the scene. (433)

The most perfect statement of the theme is the curiously titled 'Lebensweisheitspielerei' (a playing with the wisdom gained throughout life). But the pompousness of the German title in a collection of English poems, kicking against the very notion of play, asserts that even now this poet still retains a little of his earlier playfulness. And it reminds us, by thrusting the word at us in this way, that even the best suited words, even as they signal it, do some sort of damage to the meaning we are trying to convey. In other words, we can never reach the final indigence, the final misery, in life or in language. For while it is not the worst so long as we can say 'this is the worst', as Lear reminds us, it is also true that there is always a surplus, a trace of rhetoric, in even the most heartfelt expression of pain and suffering – and this too the half-jokey title subliminally conveys:

> Weaker and weaker the sunlight falls
> In the afternoon. The proud and the strong
> Have departed.
>
> Those that are left are the unaccomplished,
> The finally human,
> Natives of a dwindled sphere.
>
>
> Their indigence is an indigence
> That is the indigence of the light
> A stellar pallor that hangs on threads.
>
> Little by little, the poverty
> Of autumnal space becomes
> A look, a few words spoken.
>
> Each person completely touches us
> With what he is and as he is
> In the stale grandeur of annihilation. (429–30)

Now, in his half-asleep state, the poet can shed the persona of the aesthete or the clown he had so often adopted to protect himself from sentimentality, and trust the words and rhythms to lead him where he wants. He always knew 'that he was a spirit without a foyer', but this, he now understands, is a cause not of mourning but of celebration, for to him 'local objects become / More precious than the most precious objects of home'. No longer part of any family (his siblings all dead), no longer attached to the past ('without a remembered past, a present past, / Or present future'), alone in his room, an old man, he can dream of objects not present and grasp that:

> Little existed for him but the few things
> For which a fresh name always occurred, as if
> He wanted to make them, keep them from perishing. (473–4)

Of course, as he says in another late poem:

> One would have wanted more – more – more –
> Some true interior to which to return,
> A home against one's self, a darkness,
>
> An ease in which to live a moment's life,
> The moment of life's love and fortune,
> Free from everything else, free above all from thought.

But when he contemplates what form this would take he has to fall back on metaphor and analogy:

> It would have been like lighting a candle,
> Like leaning on the table shading one's eyes,
> And hearing a tale one wanted intensely to hear. (469)

Such a turn, which leaves one wondering which is the metaphor and which the reality, and realising that in a strange way it no longer matters, is to be found in a poem he did put into his *Collected Poems*, 'The Final Soliloquy of the Interior Paramour', a title which cunningly elides solitude and company:

Light the first light of evening, as in a room
In which we rest and, for small reason, think
The world imagined is the ultimate good.

This, he says is 'the intensest rendezvous'. But who is coming
to this rendezvous, if you are alone in a room with only your
thoughts for company? The next lines probe the mystery:

It is in that thought that we collect ourselves,
Out of all the indifferences into one thing:

Within a single thing, a single shawl
Wrapped tightly round us, since we are poor, a warmth,
A light, a power, the miraculous influence

Here, now, we forget each other and ourselves,
We feel the obscurity of an order, a whole,
A knowledge, that which arranged the rendezvous. (444)

Not for the first time in these last poems we are made to
think of late Beckett. In *Company*, Beckett's greatest and most
extended late work, he too sits alone in a room with nothing
but himself for company and out of that creates what follows.
But Beckett is always suspicious of his writing self's ability
to furnish him with company, seeing it as one more lure,
one more deflection from what is real and meaningful, the
ultimate poverty. Thus he is always seeking to track down that
ability and, if he can, destroy it. The joy of his late works is that
the balance between acceptance and denial is maintained, but
even here, in the richest and most elegiac of his late offerings,
the final gesture is one of despair that he has succumbed once
more to the lure of this fake company, a figment of his ever-
fertile imagination and writing power:

Who asks who exclaims, What visions in the shadeless dark of light and shade! Yet another still? Devising it all for company. What a further addition to company that would be! Yet another still devising it all for company. Quick leave him.

With Stevens, on the other hand, there is always the sense that in the end he accepts this as an unexpected gift, an unmitigated blessing rather than the final act of treachery. Here the metaphorical shawl, 'wrapped tightly round us', serves not to remind us of our solitude but on the contrary to make us forget ourselves and feel 'the obscurity of an order, a whole, / ... that which arranged the rendezvous' – more the loving embrace of a mother than the shudder-inducing touch of the winding-sheet:

> We make a dwelling in the evening air,
> In which being there together is enough.

Having reached this stage, he is ready to say his goodbyes to the world which had given him so much pleasure and to the poetry which had been at the centre of his life. 'The Planet on the Table' takes stock of the second: 'Ariel was glad he had written his poems', it begins. They were good he feels because though they were of course 'makings of the self', they were also 'makings of the sun'. However:

> It was not important that they survive.
> What mattered was that they should bear
> Some lineaments of character,
>
> Some affluence, if only half-perceived,
> In the poverty of their words,
> Of the planet of which they were a part. (450)

This reminds me of a key passage in Leon Wieseltier's *Kaddish*, which is both an account of the year he spent saying *kaddish*, the mourner's prayer in Orthodox Judaism, three times a day for his father, and of his search through the writings of the rabbis for the meaning of this prayer. Is the reciting of it thrice daily designed to help the mourner get through the dark days after the death of his father, or is it designed, like the Catholic prayers for the dead, to help his father's soul through Purgatory? In the end, he understands, it is neither: 'The *kaddish* is not a prayer for something. It is a proof of something. The son does not request that his father be granted a good fate. The son demonstrates why his father deserves to be granted a good fate. The son is not the advocate, the son is the evidence.'[36] That the son is there, reciting the prayer, day in day out for eleven months is proof that his father has brought him up within the tradition. Simply his presence there and his daily utterance rebounds to the father's eternal glory. Similarly Stevens now understands that the poet is not the advocate of the wondrousness of the world in which he lives, of its myriad-facetedness and of the mysterious fact that it just is; he is the evidence. And knowing that is enough.

Now, finally, he can let go. The next poem in that last collection, *The Rock*, entitled 'The River of Rivers in Connecticut', shows him leaving all behind him:

> There is a great river this side of Stygia,
> Before one comes to the first black cataracts
> And trees that lack the intelligence of trees. (451)

The river flashes in the sun and 'On its banks / No shadow walks'. At the same time the familiar sights of Connecticut show up – the steeple at Farmington glistens and the church

---

36   Leon Wieseltier, *Kaddish* (New York; 1998), p.420.

at Haddam 'shines and sways'. Frank Kermode, in an essay on these late poems, argues that Stevens in speaking here, as he always has, of the local and the particular.[37] That is the one point on which I would take issue with what is surely one of his finest essays and one which has coloured my own thinking on the subject. For it seems to me that we are no longer in the world of 'An Ordinary Evening at New Haven'. The river may not be the gloomy Styx, the classical boundary between this world and the realm of the dead, but it certainly is not 'ordinary'. Though the sun shines on it, it is a strangely silent and unpeopled place. And though it is 'this side of Styx', the very mention of the river casts a shadow, as does the way we come to it in the poem, 'Before one comes to the first black cataracts'. This is a river that 'flows nowhere, like a sea', an overwhelming force against which no ferryman can navigate his barge: 'Call it once more, a river, an unnamed flowing.' And after Styx, we know, comes Lethe, the river of ultimate forgetfulness. The narrator advances towards them both, not looking back.

But Stevens the poet has one more surprise up his sleeve. Out of the blue he presents us, in a poem unpublished in his lifetime, with a dirge to rival the greatest in the language, Shakespeare's 'Fear no more the heat of the sun' in *Cymbeline*. In 'Farewell without a Guitar' Stevens had said goodbye to poetry and its gaudy trappings, giving us not a noble rider but a riderless horse, a horse which 'walks home without a rider, / Head down.' Now we discover that though he has discarded the guitar he has kept his banjo, for the poem is entitled 'Banjo Boomer':

The mulberry is a double tree.
Mulberry, shade me, shade me awhile.

---

37 'Wallace Stevens: Dwelling Poetically in Connecticut', in Frank Kermode, *An Appetite for Poetry* (London; 1989), pp.79–96.

A white, pink, purple berry tree,
A very dark-leaved berry tree.
Mulberry, shade me, shade me awhile —

A churchyard kind of bush as well,
A silent sort of bush, as well,
Mulberry, shade me, shade me awhile.

It is a shape of life described
By another shape without a word.
Mulberry, shade me, shade me awhile.

With nothing fixed by a single word.
Mulberry, shade me, shade me awhile. (475)

*

'Imagination dead imagine', Beckett enjoined both himself and us, and Wallace Stevens, in one of the greatest of his late poems, 'The Plain Sense of Things', insists that 'the absence of the imagination had / Itself to be imagined'. Imagining forgetting is as impossible as imagining the absence of imagination, yet with the one as with the other we are hungry for that experience, feeling that if only we could reach behind our imaginings, behind our memories, we would find our true place in the world at last. This remains, however, always tantalisingly out of reach.